Secrets In The Sand

Secrets In The Sand
The Archaeology Of Cape Cod

FRED DUNFORD and GREG O'BRIEN

Foreword by John Hay

Written in cooperation with the Cape Cod Museum of Natural History,
Brewster, Massachusetts

PARNASSUS IMPRINTS
Hyannis, Massachusetts

First Edition

ISBN 0-940160-63-3

Library of Congress Catalog Card Number: 97-68074

Parnassus Imprints
30 Perseverance Way
Hyannis, MA 02601

Manufactured in Canada

To the women in our lives:
Wendy Dunford and Mary Catherine O'Brien,
who inspire the trowel and the pen

Contents

"A local past is not something we can easily dispense with."

—John Hay

Foreword

Fred Dunford, staff archaeologist at the Cape Cod Museum of Natural History, has done a great service to all those who now live in a land whose old identities, learned through close association with it, have begun to fade. The American Indians, the fishing and hunting people who were the original inhabitants, have also largely disappeared, but they have left their legacy behind them, scattered throughout the landscape.

Not long after World War II, when we had moved to Dry Hill in Brewster, I was digging in our newly planted vegetable garden. There I picked up a lovely little bird point, an arrowhead fashioned out of a piece of white quartz. So I had tangible evidence that people had roamed the woodlands and hunted here for thousands of years before any white settlers landed on these sandy shores.

Shortly after our arrival on the Cape, I heard of Charles Rennie, a man who had spent years as an amateur collector of Indian artifacts. I found evidence of his potholes at the head of Stony Brook Valley in Brewster where the alewives run in the spring. Rennie had fought in the Boer War and had retired to the old people's home in town. Upon Rennie's death, Bill Marion, a member of the board of the newly-established Cape Cod Museum of Natural History, drove to Hingham and came back with Rennie's collection, by courtesy of his daughter.

Since the museum had purchased land in the Stony Brook Valley where native peoples must have speared and netted the alewives—or herring—for thousands of years, it occurred to us to ask archaeologist Dena Dincauze of the Peabody Museum at Harvard University to study the land for possible archaeological sites. She agreed, setting in motion an archaeology program at the natural history museum that continues today. Fred Dunford would become the museum's first chief archaeologist.

We also became aware of how many native Indian sites there must have been down the length of this peninsula and how many were in danger of disappearing altogether.

Burial grounds were lost to housing developments, and countless artifacts (though still plentiful if you searched in the right places) became a great deal harder to find. Many burial sites were simply bulldozed out of the way, in ignorance of what had been there. As a result of the modern way of burying the past and ignoring its evidence, much prime history has been lost to us, and we have to look to archaeology for the best means of restoring what has perished.

Excavating the remains of ancient civilizations and their artifacts has engaged the attention of western civilization for a long time, and with spectacular results. At the same time, local efforts at revealing and understanding the very land we now occupy, have gotten less public attention and support. Fortunately, archaeological research reveals the way people who lived here thousands of years before us were able to respond and adapt to the pristine lands with which they identified themselves. Changing geography and changing patterns of living are revealed during the course of an archaeological dig. We also come closer to understanding the values of native people whose lives were inseparable from nature herself, in every mood. Not being an archaeologist myself, but only an amateur observer, I think it is of the greatest importance that we learn how to live with the land we occupy. Surely our relationship to it goes deeper than that of a society of itinerants on wheels who spend their lives driving away from where they are. If there are few farmers and fishermen left who can call on the long experience of local living to interpret land history for us, then we have to undertake it ourselves for the sake of descendants. A local past is not something we can easily dispense with, any more than we can ignore nature's eternal weather. Archaeology works at interpreting links with the past which are indispensable in comprehending the present.

Regional and local efforts to reveal and explain the archaeological record, such as the one now under the leadership of Fred Dunford of the Cape Cod Museum of Natural History, are not in the business of resurrecting dead history. We are now living at the far end of a long period of co-existence with land and sea. The evidence can be found in level after level of cultural engagement that goes back 10,000 years or more before the modern world came in to claim ownership.

We ought to reflect on this evidence, and consider the lives of native peoples who lived here thousands of years ago. Fred Dunford's wonderful book on the archaeology of Cape Cod, co-authored by Greg O'Brien, a longtime trustee of the museum, takes us back to this rich past, a journey that offers the promise of finding a better future.

John Hay
Brewster, Massachusetts

Introduction

I first met Fred Dunford about six years ago at a meeting of the Board of Trustees of the Cape Cod Museum of Natural History. The Harvard-educated Dunford presented a strong case to the board for expanding the museum's archaeology program. We were impressed.

Fred had a passion for his work beyond anyone I had ever met. His word picture of prehistoric life in Brewster's Stony Brook Valley was as colorful as a Monet painting and sparked my interest in the study of archaeology.

Archaeology is a wonderfully contagious study. Cradling in your hand a stone spear point that was carved from rock 10,000 years ago gives historical perspective new meaning. Where and how the first Cape Codders lived are questions as fundamental as the origin of the universe. The pursuit of answers offers us a chance "to turn back to the lessons of the past, in hopes of saving the future," as John Hay once wrote.

Fred and I embarked on this project in 1995, working closely as a team: Fred supplied the research and contributed to the writing of the manuscript; I shaped the material and edited the manuscript, much of it written in Fred's voice. We worked out of my studio in Brewster's rural Stony Brook Valley, where ancient stone tools and other artifacts had been found. Walking in my backyard one afternoon last spring, in an area that had been bulldozed for a new septic system, Fred, who has the eyes of a police dog, spotted a broken spear point.

"Look at this!" he said.

Fred dusted off the point, studied it for characteristic marks, then declared with understatement, "It's about 7,000 years old."

My two youngest children, Colleen, 11, and Conor, 8, were amazed.

"Daddy, do you think we can find more?" Colleen asked. "Probably," I replied cautiously, reflecting on the history of Stony Brook Valley and the fact that their friend, Daniel Wilbur, a young neighbor, had recently discovered pieces of prehistoric pottery in his backyard.

The next day as I walked from my house to the studio, I noticed two small pits about three feet wide and three feet deep. They had been excavated near the spot where Fred had found the spear point. Colleen, Conor and their friend Daniel had conducted their first official "dig."

I was pleased.

Today, it is essential to view the world with the curious eyes of a child. "We are born with an innate curiosity, with an incredible number of questions to ask," explorer Robert Ballard told me recently. "If we cease to ask questions, we lose our curiosity, or if the system is not responding to our curiosity, then a tragic thing happens: We stop asking."

Ballard's questions and curiosity led him and a team from Woods Hole Oceanographic Institution on Cape Cod to discover the famed *Titanic* in July 1986 about 500 miles off the coast of Newfoundland.

"We need to rediscover the child in all of us," Ballard said, "and in doing so ignite the imagination of the children around us."

Secrets In The Sand: The Archaeology of Cape Cod attempts to ignite the imagination and asks many questions about the past, many of them yet to be answered. It represents 14 years of the museum's research and writing on archaeology. But this is far more than a book about prehistoric stone tools, pottery and animal bones; it is a story about a people and a place. It is a book about how Cape Cod's first inhabitants adapted to an ever-changing environment that offered both opportunities and constraints. It is a layperson's primer on the process and method of archaeology and what can be learned from what archaeologists find.

Secrets In The Sand covers 10,000 years of archaeology and history on the Cape—beginning with the first Cape Codders, the Paleoindians, direct descendants of the people who entered this continent about 12,000 years ago, crossing a land bridge that once connected Asia to North America. The book details the museum's investigations into all periods of prehistory—describing excavations at Upper Mill Pond and Wing Island in Brewster, at Pochet in East Orleans, at Sandy Neck in Barnstable, and at Fort Hill in Eastham.

"If you don't know where you are, you don't know who you are," wrote essayist Wallace Stegner.

Indeed, *Secrets In The Sand* attempts to capture a sense of place.

We stand today on the horizon of our own archaeology as we ponder what people thousands of years from now will say about who we were, how we lived, and what we saved.

It is Fred's hope and mine that this book ignites or rekindles curiosity in the past and in the future. Perhaps, in time, we will better understand our own footprints, the secrets in the sand that we will leave behind.

Greg O'Brien
West Brewster, Massachusetts
June, 1997

Acknowledgments

First, we first need to acknowledge Bill Delorey, who served as executive editor on this project. Bill's insightful revisions, line editing and suggestions have made this a better book.

We also thank the following people who provided assistance in developing this manuscript: the staff of the Brewster Ladies Library; the staff of the Sturgis Library, Barnstable; Dr. Leslie Shaw and Dr. John Cross, New England Archaeology Institute, Brunswick, ME.; the staff of the Robert S. Peabody Museum of Archaeology at Phillips Academy, Andover, MA; Rick Larsen, Brewster; Timothy Lynch, Harwich; Robert N. Oldale, U.S. Geological Survey Woods Hole, who contributed the section on geology; Steven Tucker, Acting Chief Ranger, Sandy Neck Ranger staff, Barnstable; Bill Higgins, *Cape Cod Times*; Peter and Anne Lajoie, Watermark Destop Publishing in Eastham, which produced the fine maps used in this book; Roberta Furgalack for her wonderful illustrations; Janine Perry, Brewster; Richie Hall, Cape Cod Bird Club; Beth Nelson, Cape Cod Museum of Natural History, archaeology department; Susan Lindquist, Cape Cod Museum of Natural History executive director; and the entire staff of the Cape Cod Museum of Natural History.

We also thank Bill and Betina Todd for their assistance; Barb McGeorge; Peter and Scott O'Brien; Sean and Chris O'Brien; Caroline, Andrew and William Thompson; Caitlin and Martin Holmes; and David, Kate and Erin O'Brien.

In addition, we thank Jane Vollers for her splendid photography.

Finally, special thanks is overdue to our publishers at Parnassus Imprints—Wallace Exman, one of the best book editors in the business, and Walter Curley, who handles the marketing and business side of the operation.

PART ONE

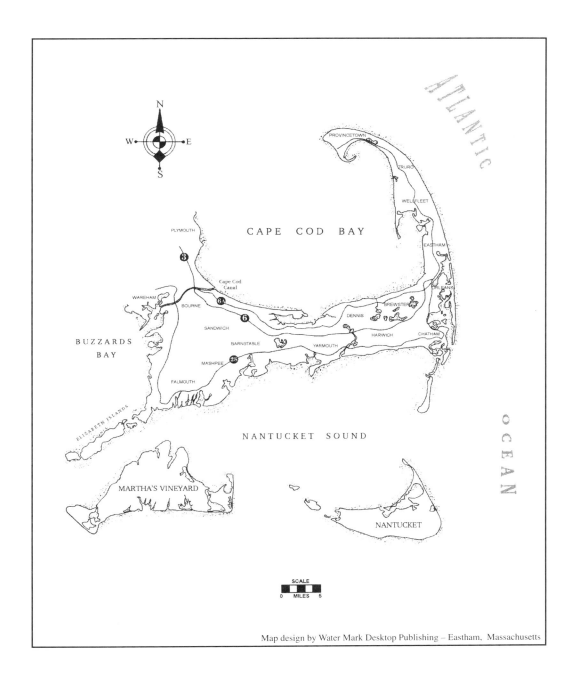

Map design by Water Mark Desktop Publishing – Eastham, Massachusetts

"A Windswept and haunting landscape."

—HENRY DAVID THOREAU

Looking Back:
A Century of Archaeology on Cape Cod

Crossing a windswept and haunting landscape he called a "constant mirage," naturalist Henry David Thoreau was drawn to the beach. "Wishing to get a better view than I had yet of the ocean, I made a visit to Cape Cod," he wrote in his classic work, *Cape Cod*. Thoreau actually made several visits to the Cape between 1849 and 1855. In his eloquent chronicle, he described the stark landscape before him as a "bended arm laid bare" by the deforestation and erosion that accompanied the European settlement of the Cape after 1620. The intensive nature of early agricultural practices and the demand for wood to build homes and ships led to the clearing of more than 31,000 acres by 1800.

But the devastating process of deforestation and erosion revealed important details about the history of the region. As wind and rain stripped the topsoil from plowed fields, stone tools and other artifacts lost their protection, offering late 19th century and early 20th century Cape Codders a chance to investigate the prehistory of the Cape.

Thoreau's journey to the ocean by coach and then on foot provides a vivid word picture of this landscape. Early in the journey, as he traveled through the north side of Dennis, he described the view from the coach window:

> We ventured to put our heads out of the windows, to see where we were going, and saw rising before us, through the mist, singular barren hills, all stricken with poverty grass, looming up as if they were in the horizon, though they were close to us, and we seemed to have got to the end of the land on that side, not withstanding that the horses were still

headed that way. Indeed, that part of Dennis which we saw was an exceedingly barren and desolate country, of a character which I can find no name for; such a surface, perhaps, as the bottom of the sea made dry land day before yesterday.

At Chatham, on the elbow of the Cape, Thoreau witnessed a similar scene:

The barren aspect of the land would hardly be believed if described. It was such soil, or rather land, as, to judge from appearances, no farmer in the interior would think of cultivating, or even fencing.

Thoreau left the coach in Orleans, and continued his journey on foot across "the plains of Nauset," a landscape he later described as "an apparently boundless plain, without tree or fence." He pondered the fertility of the plowed fields and concluded that:

The ploughed fields of the Cape look white and yellow, like a mixture of salt and Indian meal. This is called soil. All an inlander's notions of soil and fertility will be confounded by a visit to these parts, and he will not be able, for some time afterwards, to distinguish soil from sand.

Thoreau summarized his observations concerning deforestation and the Cape's meager soils, writing

The country was, for the most part, bare, or with only a little scrubby woods left on the hills . . . There is a thin layer of soil, gradually diminishing from Barnstable and Truro, where it ceases; but there are many holes and rents in this weather-beaten garment not likely to be stitched in time, which reveal the naked flesh of the Cape, and its extremity is completely bare.

It is clear from the eyewitness account of Thoreau that the Cape was indeed a barren place in the mid-19th century. But the historical record clearly shows the landscape was not always desolate. When the Plymouth colonists first explored the tip of Cape Cod in the fall of 1620, they wrote of "excellent black earth" and forests filled with "oaks, pines, sassafras, juniper, birch, holly, vines, ash and walnut."

So what happened? What first attracted the English to Cape Cod—a deep and fertile soil—was soon depleted as towns were established in Sandwich, Barnstable, Yarmouth and Eastham. At Nauset, for example, "settlers immediately began cutting down the Eastham woods, farming, and grazing their herds of cattle and sheep," naturalist Robert Finch wrote in A Guide to Nature on Cape Cod and the Islands.

By 1660, the "blackish and deep mold" of topsoil that William Bradford had originally found at Eastham was gone. . . No longer protected by the forests, the soil quickly dried out and blew away in the ever-prevalent winds. Any hardwood sprouts that began to grow back were soon grazed off by sheep, 10,000 of which were reported in Barnstable County in the late 1600s. In other words, the Eastham soil, once held and protected by the forests, was literally "gone with the wind." And without the forests, the soil could not re-form.

Similar practices took place in other Cape Cod towns, Finch wrote; as early as 1676, Sandwich created bylaws exacting fines of twelve pounds against anyone found "peeling oak" or deliberately letting wood rot.

> Housing also took its toll on the forests. In early Cape houses con-
> structed before the Cape needed to import its building material, it is common
> to find pine floorboards and wainscoting two and even three feet wide. In
> the West Parish Congregational Church on Route 6A in West Barnstable,
> a visitor can see beams of native oak sixteen inches square and forty-eight
> feet long. And in many cases the very foundations of the houses were
> made from cedar rolls, the split trunks of the great Atlantic white cedars
> that once flourished in our local wetlands.

Shipbuilding also took its toll on the forests, as farmers turned to the sea for a living after exhausting the soil. "Beginning in the late 1600s and continuing for almost a century and a half, shipbuilding was an extensive and profitable trade on the Cape," wrote Finch. " . . . the native oak and pine provided wood for many schooners, barks, whalers, and packets, as well as numerous smaller fishing vessels."

So by the time of Thoreau's historic journey across Cape Cod, the damage had been done; the "naked flesh" of the region had been exposed. While deforestation was ecologically devastating, the loss of the topsoil revealed significant details concerning the geology and history of this fragile peninsula.

In writing of his walk across the "windswept plains of Nauset" and the geology of the area, Thoreau remarked how erosion had disclosed numerous "rocks which were formerly covered with soil" appearing as if "they were recently dug from a quarry." These rocks, left by the mountainous glacier that formed Cape Cod 19,000 years ago, told of its icy birth. Elsewhere on his journey, Thoreau witnessed how erosion had unearthed other secrets in the sand: prehistoric spear and arrow points, pottery sherds and animal bones, prehistoric campsites, shell heaps, hearths and implements of the native peoples of Cape Cod, the region's first inhabitants. In Truro, for example, Thoreau saw many traces of Native American occupancy. At one site, he observed:

> Oysters, clams, cockles, and other shells, mingled with ashes and the

bones of deer and other quadrupeds. I picked up half a dozen arrow-heads, and in an hour or two could have filled my pockets with them. The Indians lived about the edges of the swamps, then probably in some instances ponds, for shelter and water.

THE ANTIQUARIANS

By the late 19th century, these secrets in the sand drew the attention of individuals who began seeking, collecting and describing these artifacts. The observations of some of these antiquarians have been passed down to us in local histories.

In the late 1880s, Harwich historian Josiah Paine visited many archaeological sites, which today have been obscured by the return of the forests or destroyed by development. In June of 1880, Paine visited the site of the last meetinghouse of the "Sauquatuckett Indians" in southwest Brewster, near what is called the Punkhorn section of town. He described the visit in his *History of Harwich,* writing that "the site was marked by a few stones and bricks, which doubtless were remains of the smoke stack, and was surrounded by young oaks of considerable height. It is reported that quite early after the commencement of the 19th century, the site was covered by tufts of grass, and that stones marked some of its corners."

In his *History of Barnstable County*, published in 1890, Simeon Deyo, referenced Yarmouth historian Charles Swift, who wrote in 1889 of "the shell heaps near the seashore and the arrow-heads and stone utensils thrown up by the passing plowshare of the husbandman, giving evidence of their numbers (native peoples) before the advent of the white man on these shores."

Historian Frederick Freeman's *History of Cape Cod*, published in 1858, included this account of the Nauset Indians, whom he suggested "occupied a prominent position" among the various tribes of the Cape:

> The principal seats of the Nauset were at Namskaket, within the present limits of Orleans, and about the cove, which divides Orleans from Eastham. At this cove, shell-fish have always been abundant, and there is still to be seen some indication of the great use they made of them, in the vast collections of shells in different places.

A keen interest in seeking and collecting artifacts and relics continued into this century. During the early 1900s, vast numbers of artifacts were unearthed along Yarmouth's Bass

Fragments of shell and animal bone at a prehistoric shell midden exposed by erosion near the shore of Cape Cod Bay. Thoreau described finding a site like this in Truro.

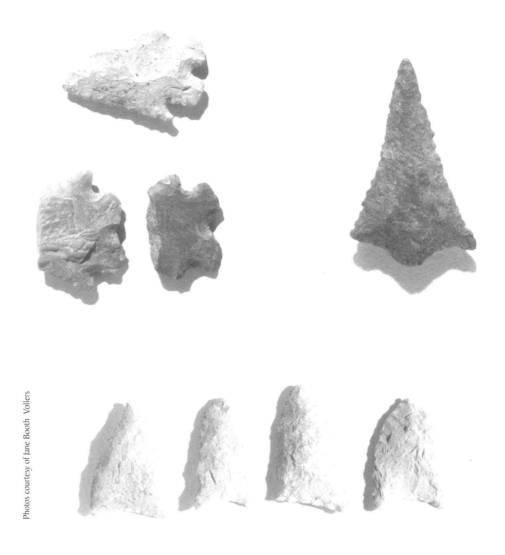

Stone spear points found by Charles Rennie in Brewster's Stony Brook Valley.

The three spear points on the upper left are about 9,500 years old—close to the time when native peoples arrived at Cape Cod. The spear point on the upper right is about 8,000 years old—similar artifacts were found during a museum excavation at Upper Mill Pond in Brewster. The spear points pictured at the bottom are about 4,000 years old. Artifacts like this have been found during the Museum's archaeological survey of Wing Island in Brewster.

River, Harwich's Herring River, Brewster's Paine's Creek, and Pleasant Bay, which straddles the eastern shores of Chatham, East Harwich, Orleans and Brewster.

Sadly, much of what was collected was never properly documented, leaving us today with thousands of artifacts, pieces of a giant puzzle jumbled in hundreds of boxes and nearly impossible to assemble.

While many of the artifacts collected in the 1800s and early 1900s have been lost to attics, barns and curiosity shops, some have been acquired by museums like ours. Since 1982 when I joined the staff here, I've had the opportunity to examine some of these collections. I have spent much time researching the notes and collections of men like the late Charles Rennie, Cleon Crowell, George and Henry Kittredge and historian Warren Sears Nickerson. These men have left us an important legacy.

The first collection I studied in the summer of 1982 belonged to Rennie, a Brewster resident who earlier in this century collected more than 6,000 artifacts, mostly stone tools, that span the entire 10,000-year prehistory of Cape Cod.

Rennie lived with his wife and two daughters several decades ago in a small house in the Stony Brook Valley of Brewster, not far from the museum. Some residents, like John Hay and Rick Larsen, still remember him.

As a boy, Larsen spent summers at a family house off Stony Brook Road, near the town's herring run. Like most of the Cape in the years following World War II, the Stony Brook Valley was thinly wooded, and much land was in cultivation, including a large field behind the Larsen family home. Larsen often saw Rennie in his later years searching for artifacts in the plowed fields, along the slopes of the valley and on the dirt roads around Brewster's mill ponds. He described Rennie as a "tall and stout man, with glasses and a bushy mustache." Rarely seen in shirtsleeves, Rennie dressed formally—even in the warmest weather—with a vest, tweed jacket and an overcoat with many pockets.

Rennie often searched the cornfields behind the Larsen house. Larsen, who was intrigued by Rennie and his hobby, frequently watched him from an upstairs window. As Rennie passed the house, he occasionally looked up at Larsen and yelled, " I'm going to look for arra-heads." Rennie's favorite time to search the cornfields was in the early morning after a rain, when the silt had been washed from ancient stone tools that lay exposed in the furrows between the rows of corn.

As Rennie headed to the fields and areas around the mill ponds, his coat pockets bulged with sandwiches and fruit to sustain him in his search, Larsen said. At the end of the day, those same pockets would carry the fruits of his labor—stone tools, arrow and spear points, stone axes, knives and plummets (teardrop-shaped stone weights used to sink fishing nets and lines).

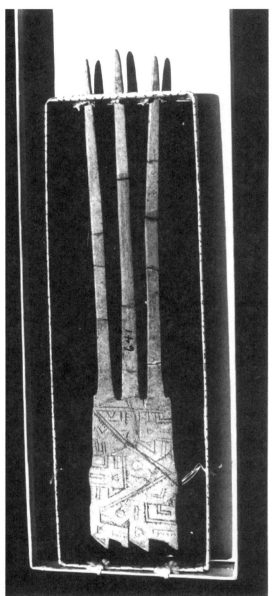

Artifacts found by Cleon Crowell.

The upper left photo shows a stone axe and a stone plummet found in Brewster's Stony Brook Valley. The photo on the right is an elaborately decorated bone comb. The decorative motif is very geometric—consisting of images of dogs or wolves' heads.

The photo on the bottom left shows fragments of a ceramic pot that Crowell partially reconstructed. The bone comb and the ceramic pot were made sometime between 1,000–400 years before present. We don't know where Crowell found these two artifacts.

Rennie also carried cloth bags, looped around his thick leather belt, that were filled with other artifacts. On his walks, he always carried a long pointed stick that he used to brush away dirt after spotting a possible artifact. At times he brought along a small hoe.

As a rare treat, Rennie invited Larsen to his house to view the artifacts, the most impressive of which were displayed in glass cases framed with pine. Other artifacts were housed in apothecary boxes with many drawers. Rennie carefully explained to Larsen and other visitors how these artifacts had been fashioned, showing his guests the battered stone hammers that had been used to shape the stone tools in his collection.

In 1969, Rennie's daughter donated a substantial part of her late father's collection to our museum. Although the collection is not documented, it offers a timeline of the prehistory of Stony Brook Valley. It contains stone implements and other artifacts from every era of the region's prehistory, including several spear points believed to be 9,500 years old, near the time when native peoples first arrived on Cape Cod. The collection also includes an important artifact from the period just before 1620 when native peoples traded with European explorers. Somewhere in Stony Brook Valley, Rennie found a small triangular copper arrow point that may have been fashioned from a sheet of copper, given in trade to a native person by a European sailor. The thousands of items in Rennie's collection attest to the large population of native peoples who once inhabited the valley.

Charles Rennie was not the only person searching the plowed fields and sandy slopes of the Stony Brook Valley for artifacts. The late Cleon Crowell of Harwich, son and business partner of famed decoy maker Elmer Crowell, was also an avid collector. While many are familiar with the artistry of Elmer and Cleon in carving working decoys, shorebirds, miniatures and ornamentals, few know that Cleon amassed one of the most significant archaeological collections ever assembled on Cape Cod. A portion of this collection, stored at the Cape Cod Museum of Natural History, offers unusual insight into the archaeology of Stony Brook Valley, Pleasant Bay at the Cape's elbow, and Barnstable's Sandy Neck.

What makes Crowell's collection so significant is its documentation. Unlike many of his contemporaries, Crowell kept a journal of what he found and created a map of where he found it. The pages of his journal, a worn hard-bound ledger, were numbered and lined. Writing in pencil and in a strong hand, Crowell described various artifacts, recorded their location and noted their significance. For example, in journal entry number 26, he described a method of prehistoric cooking by which heated rocks were placed in a clay pot to boil its liquid contents: "Cooking stone used by heating very hot in the fire and then put into pottery kettle of water. When water stops boiling another one is added. Dug from a shell heap on the north bank."

The inside cover of Crowell's journal expresses his respect for the native peoples of

Cape Cod, and his introduction reveals the precise locations where he actively searched and collected. "The Indians did not learn from books," he wrote. "Their knowledge came from past experience. . . .The Indian relics recorded in this book were made and used by the local tribes, who lived and hunted the woods and streams of southeastern Cape Cod. The tribes are known as follows: Nauset, Potanumaquut (Pot-a-nim-a-kit), Monomoyick and Sauquatucket (Sa-qua-tuck-et)."

On his map, Crowell located specific sites that he regularly explored on the Outer Cape. In a letter to his friend and neighbor, historian Warren Sears Nickerson, Crowell discussed the differences and similarities of some of these ancient sites. Wrote Crowell, "I have been doing some digging at Barley Neck [in East Orleans] and I find that the pottery is of a much better quality than they made here at Muddy Cove [on Pleasant Bay in East Harwich]. It is firmer and runs a good deal on the smooth type. Not so much the overall design. Some of these patterns are very interesting. Never saw any like them before anywhere."

Today, this pencil-drawn map, faded, worn and stained, is itself an artifact. Crowell created his map by copying a map of Native American communities and territories from Deyo's *History of Barnstable County*. Crowell used the Deyo illustration to create a base map on which he placed symbols locating his sites. The symbols Crowell selected were first used by archaeologist Warren K. Moorehead, who was then affiliated with the Robert S. Peabody Museum of Archaeology at Phillips Academy in Andover, Massachusetts. From its inception in 1901 until his retirement in 1936, Moorehead conducted numerous archaeological surveys throughout the Northeast. In the published reports of these surveys, Moorehead used various symbols to record sites he had found: a "teepee" for a campsite; an "X" for a shell midden; and a stick figure for a burial. Crowell owned a copy of these survey reports and used Moorehead's symbols to record his own site locations.

Crowell's map shows the locations of ancient campsites on both sides of Paine's Creek in the Stony Brook Valley. At one campsite in West Brewster, he found a "prehistoric bone arrow point, two bone needles [used for sewing] and a rare Indian pipe," and at sites across the creek, he discovered a grooveless stone axe and a " rare and old stone knife." Crowell in his journal described the artifact by noting, "This old knife shows signs of being worn a great deal." The entry suggests he showed the artifact to Moorehead, who identified it as a "cleverly made skinning knife."

Discovered needles made from deer bone, a pipe made from nearby clay and a stone axe were evidence of the ingenious use of natural resources by native peoples, Crowell wrote in his journal.

Like Rennie, Crowell found that the plowed fields of Stony Brook Valley were among the most fruitful places to search for artifacts. His journal provides clear evidence of his good fortune in these fields. In one entry, Crowell describes a large stone axe which had been "plowed out of the ground."

While the Stony Brook Valley was an important spot for Crowell, he spent more time collecting at Pleasant Bay near his family home in East Harwich. In *The Bay As I See It*, Crowell's friend and neighbor Nickerson described the "haunting loveliness" of Pleasant Bay:

> From the front door . . . I can overlook the whole length and breadth of The Bay. From there I see the mid-summer sun break up out of the eastern rim of the Atlantic and peer in through The Narrows, as through an open window, to waken its sleeping waters. At sundown I watched the smoky sou'wester role its blanket of fog down out of the Head of The Bay to put its waves to sleep again. And through the stillness of the night there comes up to me the soft lullaby of the incoming tide on its sandy shore.

Having grown up a short distance from the bay, Crowell was familiar with the scene and with the bay's many creeks and coves. Muddy Cove, which he called the "Monomoyick River," was of special interest to him. On his map, both shores of the cove are lined with symbols indicating the location of "wigwam sites" and "shell heaps."

Shell heaps or shell middens are refuse deposits of varying sizes that consist primarily of discarded shell, plant and animal remains, broken stone and bone tools and other household items. The presence of great quantities of shell neutralizes the acidity of the soil, preserving important information about prehistoric environments, resources and the implements made and used by native people.

Crowell's reference in his journal to "wigwam" sites on the "Monomoymick River" came from his strong belief that the river was at the heart of the "Monomoyick Tribal Lands," and that the "wigwam" sites had actually been the dwellings of tribal members. In journal entry number 686, Crowell describes his excavation of one of the wigwam sites:

> *In digging these wigwam sites, we noticed animal bones of all kinds were plenty, all kinds of birds, bones, too, more so by a large percentage than we had seen elsewhere on the Cape. This show[s] that the Indians who lived in this group of wigwams were great hunters, and their appetite for meat was greater than for clams.*

Another letter to Nickerson provides clear evidence of the prolific nature of Crowell's collecting activity at the river: "I dug out at least 15 different wigwam sites along the north bank of Muddy River and found everything from sky stones to petrified wood."

Blankets of fog still roll down out of the head of Pleasant Bay, as Warren Sears Nickerson described them.

COLLECTING ON SANDY NECK

While Charles Rennie and Cleon Crowell were busy searching the plowed fields of Stony Brook Valley and the creeks and coves of Pleasant Bay, Harvard professor George Lyman Kittredge and his son, Henry, were investigating the dunes at Sandy Neck, a six-mile long barrier beach that stretches east along the shore of Cape Cod Bay from the Sandwich town line toward Dennis. Professor Kittredge, one of the world's foremost experts on Shakespeare in his day, spent a good part of his life at the family summer home in Barnstable, often searching the dunes of Sandy Neck for artifacts. Kittredge had a passion for collecting "arrowheads and other Indian relics," according to his former student and biographer, Clyde Kenneth Hyder.

In a July 28, 1905 letter to his daughter, Frances, Professor Kittredge wrote of a search for arrowheads on Sandy Neck: "Henry & I went to Sandy Neck in the dory, took lunch & searched for arrowheads. A place near Brayley's where we never had found anything to speak [of] had blown out during the winter & was unmolested. There and elsewhere we got between 40 & 50 excellent specimens, not to speak of more dubious treasures. Henry found a large fragment of an uncommonly large pendant, his first prize of that nature."

In another letter to Frances on her birthday, Kittredge wrote of a trip to Eastham in search of more artifacts. "Yesterday, Mamma, Henry & I went down to Eastham partly for the excursion, partly to look for relics. We got a good deal of both."

Henry C. Kittredge, one of the original trustees of the Cape Cod Museum of Natural History, followed his father's passion for collecting "relics" and exploring Sandy Neck. In his boyhood diary, Henry described one of the more unique artifacts in his collection. On June 27, 1903 he wrote, "Dora came in and said that Mr. John Manley was out on the piazza with Papa. He has been out West and got a lot of Indian things. I went out to see him and he said, 'Henry, are you an archer?' I said I was out of practice. And he said, 'Well, I've a first rate Indian bow, six poisoned arrows and some arrows that are not poisoned. And I thought perhaps you might like them.'"

Another diary entry demonstrates the close relationship between father and son and the times spent together searching for artifacts. Henry wrote of sailing the family boat across Barnstable Harbor with his father to Sandy Neck. "But after a while we got over to Brailey's [sic] where we decided to land. Papa and I went ashore to look for arrowheads. We each found about seven."

When Henry was 18, he and some friends built "a gunning shanty" on the Neck. A diary entry dated March 24, 1908 describes that adventure:

"I'm going to chip in $25 for a gunning shanty on Sandy Neck. Harry Peterson is getting it up, and there are going to be six fellows— Harry Peterson; Lincoln, a fellow at school; Sunny; Alfred Redfield, a summer guy at Barnstable [and] a pretty decent lad; Henry Durant, a law student; and me. It is going to be up near Keith's shanty; its dimensions are 14 by 14 feet, stove and piazza and four bunks, besides a woodbox. Pretty nifty. One sixth share for only $25 and Pa says that."

Kittredge and the others called the joint venture the Mosquetucket Club. Alfred Redfield, a member of the group, became one of the first scientists at the prestigious Woods Hole Oceanographic Institution and spent years studying the Great Marshes that bordered Sandy Neck. His work, "Development of a New England Salt Marsh," described later in our Sandy Neck chapter, was one of the most significant salt marsh studies ever published.

While Rennie, Crowell, the Kittredges, and numerous other Cape Codders were creating important collections of prehistoric stone implements, historian Warren Sears Nickerson was collecting a different type of artifact. Nickerson, a Harwich native born in 1881 and a direct descendant of the first English settler of Chatham, developed one of the most comprehensive archives of research material about the native peoples of Cape Cod.

Nickerson relied primarily on deeds, proprietors' records and other legal instruments to describe the territorial organization of the Monomoyicks, Nawsetts and the Sauquatucketts. Writing in 1933, he described these communities:

Those Indians who inhabited the Lower Cape on the arrival of the white man seem to fall into three main groups, the Monomoyicks, the Nawsetts and the Saquatucketts. While the dividing line between these groups was not defined by metes and bounds, a Sachem's tribal domain apparently was recognized as taking in all of a certain drainage area, or water shed, and extending roughly to the height of land separating him from his neighboring Sachem's hunting ground.

Nickerson carefully reconstructed the family groups of more than 1,100 native people who lived between Yarmouth's Bass River and Wellfleet during the 17th and 18th centuries. His meticulous genealogical research allowed him to place an individual within a community, while describing the person's relationship to other individuals. For example, Nickerson offered this description of Richard Shantum of the Saquatuckett community:

Richard Shantum, so far as I know, never signed his name as Sachem, but as he pledged the fidelity of Sauquatucket to the Colony he must have been so recognized by both whites and Indians. Moreover, there is no proof in my notes that he was the son of Sampson, but his surname Shantum, together with his prominence in the Sauquatuckets, make it certain that he was of the royal blood and a descendant of Mashantampaine. The Ralph branch of Mashantampaine's family took the surname of Ralph and stuck to it, as I have said, but there is no record of a family by the surname of Sampson. Putting all these circumstances together, it is my opinion that Richard Shantum of Sauquatucket was the son of Sampson of Nobscusset. He appears to have lived most of his life at Sauquatucket, near the Mill Pond, as most of the Nobscussetts of his generation did. His land where his wigwam stood was long known as Richard's Field. There is no documentary proof of his children, but there were three and possibly a fourth—Indians of Sauquatucket—who appear to have probably been sons.

But it was the life of Mattaquason, Sachem of the Monomoyick community, that so captured Nickerson's attention. In the introduction to a story about the life and times of Mattaquason, the "Old Sagamore," Nickerson wrote:

> The life of Mattaquason of Monomoyick, the Old Sagamore, as he was familiarly known on the elbow of Cape Cod where he lived, covered an extremely interesting and difficult period in our early colonial history. He was born while yet the impact of white civilization had made no impression on the lives and customs of his people. He lived well into that period following King Philip's War, which saw his tribe being reduced to almost abject slavery and its corn lands and camp sites fast becoming the farms and villages of the hated white men.

Through his own family history, Nickerson was directly tied to Mattaquason. In 1655, Nickerson's ancestor, William Nickerson, the first English settler in the land of the Monomoyicks, "entered into a bargain with Mattaquason, the Sachem of Monomoit, concerning large tracts of land in the present towns of Chatham and Harwich. There is a tradition that while the bargain was being made, the Old Sagamore retired to his wigwam to await a sign. If a bear should come prowling around within the next few days, the deal would be off, but if a deer showed up, it would be a sign that all was well. It must have been a deer that turned the scales because the bargain stood for nearly 20 years between the red man and the white, with never a scrap of paper passed between them."

Nickerson goes on to note that his ancestor paid "the Old Sagamore a shallop, ten coats of trucking cloth, six kettles, 12 axes, 40 shillings in wampum, a hat and 12 shillings in money." He was intrigued by the notion that his ancestor William and the "Old Sagamore" peacefully lived out their days together in neighboring homes on the shores of Pleasant Bay. He described the proximity of their homes: "His [Nickerson's] house stood at the head of Ryder's Cove in Chathamport next door to the wigwam of the Old Sagamore from whom he bought his land. Here they grew old together, the white man and the red, good neighbors always."

Cape Cod Community College professor Delores Bird Carpenter recently annotated and edited several of Nickerson's unpublished papers. That work, published in *Early Encounters,* preserves a valuable record of Cape Cod History.

The important collections of artifacts and historical documents that were created by Nickerson, Rennie, Crowell, the Kittredges and many other New Englanders were indeed the pieces of a giant puzzle, which when finally assembled, would reveal images of the long history of New England's native peoples.

ASSEMBLING THE PUZZLE

By the early 1930s, the science of archaeology was beginning to develop in New England. Formally trained archaeologists, working with self-taught amateurs, began developing a framework within which the pieces of the puzzle could be properly assembled. Writing in 1935, Charles C. Willoughby, Director Emeritus of Harvard's Peabody Museum, described these initial efforts: "It is only during the last few years that systematic research has been undertaken into the archaeology of the region by our larger museums and scientific institutions, and by a few individuals of means."

Essentially, these early archaeologists were trying to create a timeline of the region's prehistory by systematically sorting the thousands of artifacts stored in museums and in the cabinets of historical societies into groupings that represented the various periods of native occupation in the region before 1620.

In his book, *Antiquities of the New England Indians,* published in 1935, Willoughby offered his own timeline of the region's prehistory. It was divided into two simple periods: Algonkian and Pre-Algonkian. The divisions, he wrote, were determined by examining the economy, technology and burial practices of each of these cultures. The Pre-Algonkian native peoples were the first to occupy New England. These people, Willoughby wrote, were hunters who "used the Eskimo type of bird spear with side prongs, also the semi-lunar knife and many types of slate projectile points now found only among boreal tribes."

Their successors, the Algonkians, he declared, were farmers, who were separated into "early and late" groups, according to the shape of their ceramic vessels. While Willoughby's attempt at creating an historical framework was significant for its time, it was too broad and did not take regional variations into consideration.

By the mid-1940s in Massachusetts, there was a growing concern among archaeologists that efforts to create accurate chronological groupings of the region's artifacts had failed. As a result, archaeologists working in Massachusetts could not effectively classify artifacts from their excavated sites or from museum or private collections. While thousands of artifacts had been collected, they had yet to be organized in a way that would reveal important details about the region's prehistory. Simply stated, the pieces of the puzzle remained jumbled in countless boxes—the picture of the past was incomplete. But this soon changed.

The Massachusetts Archaeological Society called a meeting of its Research Council in January of 1945 to develop a strategy for creating a framework that ultimately would organize the stages of the region's prehistory. At that meeting, archaeologist Ripley Bullen reviewed five prehistoric archaeological sites which showed clear evidence of undisturbed stratigraphy—that is, layers of occupation within these sites had not been disturbed by plowing, erosion, construction or vandalism. This was a significant observation. A general rule in archaeology states that in undisturbed sites the deepest stratum (layer) of occupation is the oldest and the top stratum represents the most recent occupation. Simply put, the layers of each site provide evidence of specific groups of people living at specific periods of time.

When undisturbed sites like the ones reviewed by Bullen are carefully excavated, archaeologists can sort the recovered artifacts into distinct groups or assemblages, which show how people lived during these periods of time. By creating a chronological sequence of assemblages, archaeologists can show how change occurred over time. The next step—and a far more difficult one—is to explain why change happened.

At the research council meeting, Bullen stressed that archaeologists working in Massachusetts should pursue a plan of identifying and excavating sites that had undisturbed stratigraphy in an effort to determine the stages in the region's prehistory. The council agreed and then issued a directive for the careful, scientific excavation of undisturbed archaeological sites across the state. Archaeologists at last had a plan for creating a framework of the region's prehistory. The puzzle could now be assembled.

Three years after that historic meeting, Bullen concluded that "sufficient work has been done in eastern Massachusetts" to justify comment on how and why change occurred within the prehistoric societies of southern New England. Bullen, who carefully studied both stone tools and ceramic sherds from undisturbed sites in eastern Massachusetts, suggested that certain cultural changes resulted from interaction with native communities from outside southern New England. Other changes, he said, were the result of local innovations and adaptations. In general, Bullen concluded, there was "gradual cultural change with time."

With this framework in place, Massachusetts archaeologists began to explore variations in the archaeological record across the state to see if there were cultural differences between prehistoric coastal and inland communities.

A stone spear point—about 4,000 years old, found during the Cape Cod Museum of Natural History's archaeological survey of Wing Island. Artifacts like this were the focus of the "pensive figure" in Moffett's lithograph "Man Hunting Arrowheads."

THE ELUSIVE ARROWHEAD

Meanwhile, renowned Provincetown artist Ross Moffett, an early proponent of Modernism, had been carefully investigating and recording prehistoric archaeological sites on Outer Cape Cod. "He was, quite simply, searching the terrain for the elusive arrowhead, a sherd of past civilizations which became, for him, an intense preoccupation, especially during the period between 1947 and 1953," wrote friend and biographer Josephine Del Deo.

Moffett captured the spirit of his search in a lithograph entitled, *Man Hunting Arrow-heads,* in which a pensive figure, head bent toward the ground, searched for the "elusive arrowhead." Moffett's "archaeological studies and preoccupations were unavoidably re-flected in his painting," Del Deo wrote. She described Moffett's still life painting entitled, "The Artists Geology Lesson," as perfectly combining "the two disciplines—archaeology and art."

A prominent member of the American art scene, Moffett also was closely connected to the regional archaeological community. He was a member of the Research Council of the Massachusetts Archaeological Society and a friend and frequent correspondent of Frederick Johnson, director of the R.S. Peabody Museum for Archaeology. Although Moffett was an avocational archaeologist, his field methods and published research met or exceeded the standards of the day. Bullen noted that Moffett's observations concerning several sites on the Outer Cape were essential in the development of his 1948 framework for regional prehistory.

By 1951, Moffett's knowledge of the local archaeological record was complete enough to offer thoughtful comparisons between the archaeology of Cape Cod and other parts of eastern Massachusetts. In a paper published in *American Antiquity,* Moffett wrote of a site in Truro: "Although the primary aim is to give a factual picture of the site [the Rose Site] some idea may also be conveyed of the general archaeology of this isolated area, which exhibits cultural shadings differing somewhat from those of the rest of eastern Massachu-setts."

Moffett, whose collection is housed at the R.S. Peabody Museum for Archaeology, developed an important data base for Cape Cod, and in 1957 he published a significant review of the archaeology of the Cape in which he concluded: "From this information we have been able to build up what seems for lower Cape Cod, and probably also for the whole Cape, an essentially correct idea of the sequential stages of native culture, starting in pre-ceramic times and ending in the historic period."

Moffett's "Review of Cape Cod Archaeology" stands alone today as the only synthesis of the archaeology of Cape Cod. After completing his review, Moffett turned his energy toward efforts to include the Outer Cape Province Lands within the boundaries of the proposed Cape Cod National Seashore Park.

In 1962, Moffett became the National Seashore's first official archaeologist, three years after he and biographer Del Deo formed a group called The Emergency Committee for the Preservation of the Province Lands. Moffett formed the group, "fearing that his beloved Province Lands—3,000 acres of virgin dunes and seashore [on the Truro-Provincetown line]—would wind up under the backhoe," Lisa Rose Beade wrote in a recent piece on Moffett in the magazine *Cape Cod Life*. "They [Moffett and Del Deo] worked night and day on this daunting battle, mobilizing all the forces at their disposal. Both were involved with writing and organizing to save the back shore, but it was Moffett's archaeological expertise, his commitment to conservation, and his concise, restrained and yet passionately delivered arguments that saved the virgin back shore dunes from asphalt and high rises."

On April 10, 1965, Moffet gave perhaps one of his most important lectures on the archaeology of Cape Cod. Speaking before the Massachusetts Archaeology Society, he reviewed his research from the Outer Cape and laid out his framework for reconstructing the prehistory of Cape Cod. The research was of interest to several members of the Cape Cod chapter of the Massachusetts Archaeological Society (MAS). The Cape chapter was relatively new at that time, but by the early 1970s, the group was conducting an important excavation at a shell midden site near the shore of Ryder's Cove in Chatham.

In a report published after the Ryder's Cove excavation, authors Marie Eteson, Marilyn Crary and Mary Chase shed yet more light on the prehistory of Cape Cod.

"The [Ryder's Cove area] was probably occupied during autumn and early winter by small family groups who returned yearly after the harvest to take advantage of the location ideally near to shellfish beds, migrating flocks of birds, and the few deer browsing around Great Hill," the report said. "From our shellfish remains, we know that the water was at least as warm as it is now . . . Our own experience on site indicates that a winter camp could have been quite livable."

In the summer of 1979, one year after the Cape Cod chapter of the MAS published the results of its excavation, archaeologists from the National Park Service began the most ambitious archaeological project ever undertaken on the Cape. Dr. Francis P. McManamon was given the task of conducting an archaeological survey of the Cape Cod National Seashore to locate and examine both prehistoric and historic archaeological sites. The project, given the acronym CACO, continued until 1984. Much of the groundwork for the project—the mapping and recording of known sites—had been done years before by Moffett.

"The general goal of the survey was the inventory and assessment of archaeological resources within the Seashore in order to provide for their effective management," McManamon wrote in an introduction to his report. "Effective management involves the preservation and accurate interpretation of the important archaeological resources in the Seashore."

As you will see in the chapters to come, locating buried archaeological sites is a needle-in-a-haystack proposition. You can randomly search the haystack, hoping to find the needle, or you can systematically search the haystack, with a plan that increases the probability of finding the needle. Thus, when archaeologists search for artifacts and features within known sites, they use a variety of sampling strategies that increases the probability of finding artifacts and features.

Imagine the challenge of searching a national seashore of more then 22,000 acres. But McManamon countered this difficulty by designing what proved to be an extremely effective plan for locating archeological sites. He reviewed the work of geologists and other earth scientists to reconstruct the topography of the Cape thousands of years ago. He then divided the Park into areas likely to contain sites (such as salt marshes, freshwater ponds and wetlands, which provided important resources for native peoples) and places not likely to contain sites (areas far from the resources of bays, saltmarshes and freshwater). McManamon and his project managers randomly selected survey test units within the areas and began the search for sites.

In all, more than 200 sites were identified, and several of them were carefully examined, including campsites and shell middens at High Head in Truro, and Eastham's Salt Pond and Fort Hill. During the summers of 1980 and 1981, I was fortunate to be a part of the project. In fact, most of the field methods I use today and teach to my own students, I learned during that project.

The CACO project had two important results. First, the comprehensive nature of the search for archaeological sites (thousands of shovel test pits) allowed McManamon to identify the most archaeologically sensitive areas within the Park, resulting in the effective management of the Park's archaeological resources. Secondly, the results of McManomon's survey provided important insights into lifeways of the native peoples of Cape Cod.

Results of the CACO project showed that as the salt marshes developed 3,000 years ago in estuaries like Nauset Inlet near Fort Hill in Eastham, large settlements were established in these areas. The project's careful examination of plant and animal remains from shell middens at the estuaries confirmed the importance of coastal resources for native peoples.

But the most striking find during the CACO project occurred outside the boundaries of the Cape Cod National Seashore—at a construction site in Wellfleet near Cape Cod Bay.

In September, 1979, archaeologists working on the CACO project were called to the construction site where a backhoe operator had disturbed a prehistoric burial site while excavating a hole for a septic system. McManamon and Dr. James Bradley of the Massachusetts Historical Commission determined that the skeletal remains were part of a prehistoric burial feature called an "ossuary," a type of burial site that typically contains the remains of a number of individuals—men, women and children of various ages. Archaeologists believe ossuaries, which are exceptionally rare in New England, were created by communities to reaffirm the kinship and family relationships of their members. McManamon and Bradley carefully excavated the undisturbed portion of the ossuary, describing the site in a report, published by the National Park Service:

> The burial feature was composed of a thick layer of unburned and disarticulated human skeletal material . . . . Beneath this bone layer was another layer of human bone that had been burned intensely as part of a cremation. Although at quick glance the burial appeared to be a jumbled and disorganized mass of bone, there was evidence of internal organization.

After the excavation was completed, the skeletal remains were examined by a physical anthropologist, Dr. Anne Magennis. She concluded that the ossuary held the remains of 56 individuals—adult males, adult females and several children, some less than six months old.

> Examination of the bones revealed that the population represented had been a remarkably healthy one," the report said. "There was little evidence of disease-related pathology and no unusual incidence of trauma. Contrary to initial popular speculations that mass burial might have resulted from evidence or other catastrophic occurrence, the burial feature represents the mortuary practice or a particular group in which all or most of those who died within a period of time were buried together ceremonially.

After completing the analysis of the skeletons, the remains were returned to the local Native American community for reburial. While the accidental discovery of the ossuary was a striking find, archaeologists still do not know what led native communities on Outer Cape Cod to adopt that practice about 1,000 years ago.

The discovery of the Wellfleet ossuary underscores the nature of archaeology on Cape Cod. Since Thoreau's trek across the Cape, the efforts of antiquarians and archaeologists have significantly advanced our understanding of the prehistory of the region. But there is still much to be learned. Each intriguing discovery raises new questions. In the pages that follow, we attempt to answer these and other questions, understanding all along that archaeologists have barely scratched the surface.

"*Change is the coin of this sandy realm.*"

——ROBERT FINCH, THE PRIMAL PLACE

First People
of the Narrow Land

When the Pilgrims first stepped upon the shores of Cape Cod Bay in the cold, forbidding November of 1620, they found not a New World but an old one—an ancient landscape that bore the traces of 10,000 years of human endeavor. Fields, gardens, villages and well-worn paths had been etched indelibly into a mosaic of environments that in 1620 defined Cape Cod.

As these visitors traversed the area that is now Provincetown, Truro, Wellfleet and Eastham, they encountered abundant evidence of the native peoples who had wrought a successful existence from this land. At various places they found circular dwellings framed with bent saplings and covered with mats of grasses harvested from nearby marshes. Within these dwellings, they discovered the trappings and artistry of a culture uniquely adapted to the estuaries and woodlands of Cape Cod: Sturdy earthen pots and fine baskets woven from salt grasses held quantities of seeds, acorns, dried fish, and venison. There were also stores of antlers, talons, deer hooves, tobacco, milkweed, sedges, and bulrushes. Wooden bowls, dishes and trays had been carved from cedar.

Undoubtedly, the colonists were surprised to find several worn iron kettles, evidence that others from Europe, probably fishermen, had preceded them. While the native peoples of Cape Cod had so efficiently procured the resources of their environment, they had also sought and used the fruits of European contact, unaware at the time that they stood on the threshold of cataclysmic change. European settlement would bring disease and exploitation, devastating the foundation of native lifeways begun thousands of years earlier when the first bands of hunter-gatherers crossed the wind swept landscape that would, with time, become Cape Cod.

DISCOVERY

When native peoples arrived at Cape Cod about 10,000 years ago, moving northward from the south, they found an environment entirely different from that of today. The land stretched as far south as the present day islands of Nantucket and Martha's Vineyard, a gently rolling landscape of open pine forests and grasslands that had succeeded the early post-glacial forests and tundra. The area that is now Nantucket Sound was a vast expanse laced with rivers and bogs, soon to be drowned by the rapidly rising Atlantic.

Who were these people who settled on this landscape 10,000 years ago?

Their story does not begin here on this fragile, sandy peninsula, but instead thousands of miles to the northwest, at Beringia (now the Aleutians), where a narrow land bridge that once brought people to the New World now lies submerged beneath the icy waters of the Bering Strait. Approximately 12,000 years ago, near the end of the Pleistocene or Ice Age, global sea levels were much lower than present, creating land bridges in some places between the continents. Geologists suggest that the Bering Strait land bridge may have been exposed between 11,000–12,000 years ago, providing a narrow window of opportunity for small bands of hunter-gatherers who had crossed the wind swept steppes of Siberia to enter North America. Within a thousand years, these people, now called "Paleoindians" by archaeologists (from Paleolithic-Old Stone Age and Indian), had colonized all of North and South America, creating a most perplexing problem for archaeologists: What drove this migration and how did it occur? And was this, indeed, the first time that people had entered the New World?

Paleoindians moved frequently, and likely covered several hundred miles in a single year. Their mobility was essential for coping with the vagaries of resource availability in a world that was unpredictable and constantly changing. Their tool kits contained finely flaked stone knives and spear points, as well as stone scrapers for cleaning hides and burins for carving wood and bone.

On Cape Cod, we have only a fleeting glimpse of these Paleoindians, who traveled in small, highly mobile bands and left few traces of their presence. Many sites likely inhabited by Paleoindians were flooded thousands of years ago by a rising sea, leaving us with more questions than answers.

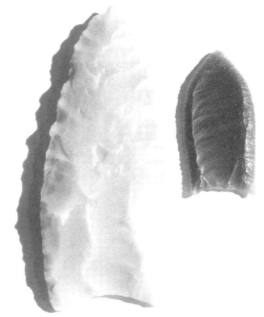

Photo courtesy of Jane Booth Vollers

Illustrations of fluted points, the classic Paleoindian artifact.

The photograph at top shows a replica of a Clovis spear point (left) and a Folsom spear point (right). These artifacts were named for the place where they were found—Clovis and Folsom, New Mexico.

The drawing below illustrates the channel-like flake on the face of the blade. That flake, or flute, is the diagnostic feature of the Clovis and Folsom spear points.

Illustration courtesy of Roberta Furgalack

PALEOINDIANS

The first Paleoindian sites were found earlier in this century in New Mexico, when American archaeology was in its infancy and little was known about the origins of Native Americans. While there had been more than one hundred years of often interesting and fanciful speculation concerning the issue, few imagined that the history of the native peoples of the Americas stretched back thousands of years to a time when the last great ice sheets were retreating northward, and mammoth, mastodon, giant bison, and other Pleistocene animals still roamed the continent.

But all that changed during the 1920's when, at Clovis and Folsom in New Mexico, finely-crafted spear points were found in direct association with Pleistocene animals, providing indisputable evidence that Native Americans had arrived here during the closing days of the last ice age. While the evidence placed Paleoindians in the ice age, it also shed light on how they lived. These early sites were actually "kill sites," places where skillful hunters armed with spears, banded together in the organized hunting of large animals. A comprehensive knowledge of the habits of their prey and the characteristics of the local terrain allowed these hunters to drive animals, like bison, towards the edge of scarps or cliffs where the animals were killed or injured as they fell. In other instances, they were herded toward gullies or arroyos where once trapped they were killed. Other species like mammoth or mastodon were stalked and driven to low-lying wetlands, where, mired in the peat, they became easy prey. After the hunt, these animals were butchered, providing significant resources for these small bands of hunters. Hides, sinew, bone, ivory and, of course, meat were carefully procured with stone scrapers and knives.

Following the discoveries at Folsom and Clovis, new Paleoindian sites were identified across the Southwest, the high plains, and on the Rocky Mountains. The excavation of these highly visible and impressive "kill-sites" greatly influenced the way archaeologists viewed the lifeways of Paleoindians.

These were indeed hunters. The artifact that characterized Paleoindian toolkits was the *fluted* spear point. A *fluted* point is a bifacially flaked (flaked on both sides) spear or projectile point, with a flake scar usually on both faces of the blade. The flake starts at the base of the point and extends toward the mid-point of the blade. Some archaeologists have argued that once impaled, a *grooved* blade caused animals to bleed excessively, which was critical in subduing animals much larger than the hunter. Some have suggested that flaking a blade in this manner was part of the process of hafting, or connecting, the blade to the shaft of the spear. Others have insisted that fluting a spear or projectile point was simply part of the broader lithic technology (stone tool technology) of Paleoindians, a trait consistent within Paleoindian groups across the continent. Clearly, any discussion about fluted point technology is central to the notion that Paleoindian life was focused on finding, following and hunting Pleistocene animals.

Paleoindians traveled in small groups of related families, a form of social organization that anthropologists call *bands*. Bands were egalitarian in nature (without formal leadership), and relatively small—perhaps ten families or slightly more. Band membership was fluid, with groups coalescing at certain times of year. Each band was highly mobile, traveling several hundred miles annually, but this was not aimless wandering. Instead, Paleoindian bands moved in an organized fashion across the landscape to places they knew contained the resources they needed—stone for tools, animals to hunt, fresh water, edible plants, and a wide variety of other life essentials. Some researchers have suggested that each band occupied and moved through socially-defined territories, areas they controlled to some extent. Territoriality, while loosely defined, may have been an important part of the Paleoindian migration. As the population grew, new bands formed and new areas were occupied.

Some archaeologists speculate that at certain times of the year neighboring bands would gather at pre-determined locations. These gatherings may have provided opportunities for groups of Paleoindians to collectively hunt herd animals like bison. In the cold winter, meat could be stored for weeks; hides would be dressed for clothing; sinew was used to haft blades to wooden shafts; and bones stripped from carcasses would be used as tools.

But the social nature of these occasions may have been more important than the hunt itself. During time spent together, band members could share valuable information about the landscape they had crossed in their travels. The shared knowledge about the environment may have been even more essential to these people than the finely-crafted spears they carried. These occasions were festive times when friendships were established or renewed, and family members living apart were reunited. Gifts were exchanged and stories told.

The archaeological record indicates that by about 11,000 years ago, migrating bands of Paleoindians had crossed the waters of the Mississippi, but the archaeological record of Paleoindian life east of the Mississippi is far different from that of the West. For example, no direct association has been established yet between Paleoindian artifacts and the bones of Pleistocene animals. The climate at this time was rapidly warming; these more temperate conditions were not suitable for mammoths, mastodons or other ice age animals. Consequently, these animals may have been close to extinction, and therefore would not have been a significant food source.

Most archaeologists who study Paleoindian lifeways agree that the specialized hunting of Pleistocene animals did not occur in eastern North America. Paleoindians in the east were confronted with an ecologically diverse and patchy landscape, which demanded new strategies for finding food and other resources. Professor Dena Dincauze of the Department of Anthropology at the University of Massachusetts and her associate, Dr. Mary Lou Curran, have argued that Paleoindians in the East were generalists who pursued a wide variety of seasonally available foods—from nuts and berries to the white tail deer. Within a few hundred years of crossing the Mississippi, the Paleoindian migration spanned the entire eastern coast, from Florida to Nova Scotia.

PALEOINDIANS ON CAPE COD: THE ENVIRONMENT

By approximately 10,000 years ago, the post-glacial climate of what was to become southern New England was even more temperate. The vegetation of Cape Cod and the exposed continental shelf was now a patchwork of open pine forests, grasslands and freshwater wetlands. Drainages flowed from headwaters on the Cape southward and eastward toward the rising Atlantic. Overall, this was a far more diverse landscape than inland areas just to the west, a fact that may have been important in the initial settlement of Cape Cod.

The retreat of the ice from southern New England and the warming, post-glacial climate led to rising sea levels, and drowned once accessible low-lying areas like Nantucket Sound, creating a series of coastal environments that were always in transition. The changing climate led to the northward migration of various plant and animal species that had been displaced by the advancing ice. Clearly, the landscape traversed by the region's first inhabitants was significantly different than it is at present.

To reconstruct this environment, archaeologists have worked cooperatively with colleagues in other disciplines, such as geology and palynology, to develop the environmental history of the region. Palynologists explore the relationship between climate and the environment by examining historical changes in forest composition. To do this, they collect and study pollen grains that have been trapped within the sediments of ponds, bogs and marshes. The surface waters of wetlands and ponds act as natural *sinks,* collecting pollen grains as they are deposited by wind or rain (picture the green residue that covers the surface of a puddle after a spring shower). The preservation of fossil pollen grains in wetland sediments provides an important data base for examining climatic and environmental change.

Long-term climatic change affects what grows in the forest because climate determines the length of the growing season. If the climate warms sufficiently to extend the growing season, then over time there may be a northward migration of certain plant species. While many other factors affect migration or range expansion, it is essential that changes in regional forest composition can be historically documented.

The vegetation of a region also is affected by human activity. The creation of fields and gardens, or manipulation of the landscape by fire, will leave an indelible signature in the pollen record for palynologists to study. For example, many pollen histories in southern New England show a significant increase in the pollen of certain grass species dated to the seventeenth century. Researchers believe this phenomenon is directly related to the European settlement of the region.

Whether the result of cultural processes or climatic change, a region's vegetation history rests with minute grains of pollen preserved deep within the sediments of marshes, bogs and pond bottoms.

To retrieve samples of pollen for study, palynologists use a piston-and-barrel-like instrument to take a core sample of a pond bottom, salt marsh, or other wetland that they think provides conditions suitable for the preservation of pollen. The coring instrument is driven, often manually, into the sediments in measured sections, usually one meter. The coring continues until palynologists are confident that they have reached the bottom of the sediments.

Sections of the core are then packaged, labeled and returned to the laboratory for study. There, macro-fossils (roots, stems and seeds) are carefully extracted from the sediment for identification. When possible, organic matter suitable for radiocarbon dating is sought within each segment of the core. Finally, acid solutions are used to dissolve the remaining material, and the pollen grains are collected for analysis. The pollen grains are counted and percentages of species present within the sample are developed. In this manner, palynologists are able to characterize plant communities that define each dated section (pollen zone) of the core. Once the dated sections are arranged in sequence, the vegetation history of the region is established.

On Cape Cod, this has been done successfully at a number of locations, including Duck Pond in Wellfleet and Owl Pond in Brewster. The interpretation of those cores provides a regional record of environmental change from 12,000 years ago to the present. For example, the pollen stratigraphy developed from the core taken at Owl Pond in Brewster by palynologists from Brown University clearly shows that at 10,000 years ago, when the Cape was first occupied, the plant communities of the region were dominated by pine species, particularly white pine.

In addition to identifying historical changes in forest composition, archaeologists use sea level curves developed by geologists to indicate the location of shorelines and marine environments at given points in time. A sea level curve is derived from dated cores taken in salt marsh peat. Because salt marshes grow at sea level, the rate of sea level rise can be derived from the oldest dated salt marsh peats. These curves can be used to reconstruct the rate of sea level rise. For archaeologists, they are useful devices for approximating the

Approximate shoreline at 10,000 yrs. B.P.

ATLANTIC

OCEAN

SCALE
0   MILES   5

B.P. = YEARS BEFORE PRESENT

Created with the assistance of:
Robert N. Oldale (U.S. Geological Survey) and Dr. Elazar Uchupi (Woods Hole Oceanographic Institution)

Map design by Water Mark Desktop Publishing – Eastham, Massachusetts

location of shoreline and marine environments thousands of years ago. Note the illustration developed with USGS geologist Oldale and Dr. Eleazar Uchupi at the Woods Hole Oceanographic Institution, that indicates the approximate location of the shoreline of Cape Cod when Native Americans first entered the region 10,000 years ago.

By working with our colleagues in the earth sciences, we are able to visualize the landscape inhabited by native peoples thousands of years ago, and in so doing, learn something about their adaptation to these fragile outposts.

PALEOINDIANS ON CAPE COD: THE ARCHAEOLOGICAL EVIDENCE

Archaeological evidence from several well-known sites in New England, e.g., Bull Brook on the north shore of Massachusetts and the Vail site in central Maine, clearly indicates that between 10,000–11,0000 years ago, the Paleoindian migration had reached New England. But evidence for the presence of Paleoindians on Cape Cod is very elusive. Why?

Several factors have made it difficult for archaeologists to discover evidence of Paleoindians on Cape Cod. First, sea level has risen approximately 50 meters (about 150 feet) during the last 10,000 years, drowning low-lying areas that may have contained Paleoindian camp sites. Secondly, Paleoindians lived in fairly small, highly mobile groups that moved frequently. The evidence of their movement across the landscape is minimal, with the exception of large camps like Bull Brook, where bands of Paleoindians came together year after year.

However, while a fluted point, the type artifact that defines the Paleoindian migration, has not been found on Cape Cod, several stone spear points, which most researchers agree date to the late Paleoindian Period (9,500–10,000 years ago) have been found here. These spear points are typically long, narrow and very thin, exhibiting exceptionally fine parallel flaking on both faces of the blade. Spear points like this have been found at sites throughout New England. On Cape Cod, artifacts like this have been found in several locations, but the most remarkable discovery occurred more than forty years ago when Tim Lynch and his family, found a cache of these spear points beneath the roots of an overturned tree on the western shore of Bass River.

A MAGNIFICENT FIND

Tim Lynch, a Harvard-trained anthropologist, remembers the first time he held an artifact. "A music teacher in the seventh grade gave me a collection of spear points that her father, an old school master, had given her," he recalls. Lynch was mystified as he held the points

Late Paleoindian Period spear points from Cape Cod.

This significant cache of spear points was found by Tim Lynch and his family at Bass River in Yarmouth in the 1950s. These spear points are very thin and exhibit exceptionally fine parallel flaking on both faces of the blade. They are characteristic of the late Paleoindian Period in southern New England.

and ran his fingers up and down the sharp, flaked edges. He tried to imagine, as many of us have done, what life was like thousands of years ago. From that moment on, Lynch was devoted to the study of archaeology. He began devouring articles on the subject and spent much of his free time surface picking and digging for artifacts along Bass River in South Yarmouth near his home. His interest in archaeology carried over into adulthood.

For 23 years, Lynch taught ancient history at Harwich High School. He was, in fact, my ninth grade ancient history teacher and kindled my interest in archaeology. He became a friend and mentor, taking my classmates and me on an excavation, bringing us to museums and sharing his love of archaeology with all who were lucky enough to have him as a teacher.

Since the early 1950s, Lynch has walked the fertile grounds of Bass River, scouring for artifacts on the westerly side just north of High Bank Road Bridge. Over the years, he has found an assortment of broken spear points, pieces of prehistoric pottery, a grooved stone axe, antler fragments and the teeth of a wolf.

"It was free picking in the early days," says Lynch, a tall, sturdy man in his late fifties. "It was wild land. Today what is left of any artifacts is buried beneath the well-manicured lawns and paved roads of subdivisions in the area."

Lynch's most impressive discovery—and what may be the most significant archaeological discovery to date on Cape Cod—occurred when he was in the ninth grade, late in September when he was taking his usual weekend foray along Bass River with his mother, brother and sister. "We cut through a little triangular patch of woodland on the westerly side of Bass River, southwest of a huge glacial boulder called Blue Rock," he recalls. "A very old pine tree had been blown over in a storm, kicking up a large amount of soil that had been under the root system. My eyes were drawn to the ground where I spotted an old projectile point that had once been attached to a now decayed wooden shaft. The point was about three inches long and about two inches wide at the base."

Lynch's brother immediately dropped to his knees and found two more points in the loose sand. "My sister also instinctively dropped to her knees and began scooping up handfuls of loose dirt like a miniature bucket loader. Sifting through the soil, she recovered a cache of nine points. We were euphoric! We gingerly wrapped the points in cloth and raced home to show my father, who was a school superintendent at the time."

The points were in perfect condition with the exception of one that had snapped in half. Impressed by what he saw, Lynch's father suggested they try to determine the age of the 12 points. Lynch's brother, who was a student at Harvard, took them to a professor at Harvard's Peabody Museum. The professor said the points had been flaked from Kineo felsite—a grey-green igneous rock containing feldspar and quartz crystals found in Maine.

The professor theorized that the felsite was dragged here 19,000 years ago by the glacier or that native people here had traded with someone near Mt. Kineo for the points. "Other than saying the points were very old, the professor could not date them precisely," says Lynch, who still displays the artifacts.

More than confirming that Paleoindians had arrived on Cape Cod sometime around 10,000 years ago, Lynch's discovery provides insight into the routes that these pioneers may have followed on their travels through the region.

By 10,000 years ago, sea level had risen to a point that placed the waters of the Atlantic and Cape Cod Bay relatively close to the Cape. Because the water table or aquifer of Cape Cod rests close to sea level, low-lying areas like Bass River in Yarmouth, Herring River in Harwich and Brewster's Stony Brook Valley may have become freshwater wetlands as sea level rose and flooded these places. If that indeed happened, these valleys would have been very attractive areas, providing Paleoindians with both plant and animal resources. In addition, these valleys may have acted as corridors for Paleoindians moving seasonally between the Atlantic shoreline to the south and the shore of Cape Cod Bay to the north.

By 9,500 years ago, the Paleoindian migration was over. The post-glacial climate continued to warm, bringing important environmental changes to the region, changes measured not in seasons but in centuries. The archaeological record of Cape Cod indicates that after 9,500 years ago, the Cape was continuously occupied by native peoples.

The effort by archaeologists in the 1930s and 1940s to create a chronological framework to organize archaeological evidence of the region's prehistory led to the creation of two major cultural periods that followed the Paleoindian migration. Each period is defined by certain economic and technological traits. The Archaic Period spans the millennia between 9,500 to about 2,500 years and is divided by early, middle and late periods. The Woodland Period covers the years between 2,500 to about 500 years ago and is similarly divided. Native peoples who lived in the region during the Archaic Period were hunter-gatherer-fishers. During the Woodland Period, agriculture was added to the subsistence base.

THE ARCHAIC PERIOD ON CAPE COD

By 8,000 years ago, sea level was about 25 meters (75 feet) lower than at present, and the low-lying area between Cape Cod and the Islands was submerged, separating the Islands from Cape Cod. (Note the illustration developed with Oldale and Uchupi.) In addition, there were important changes in forest composition. By that time, the woodlands of Cape Cod consisted of a mix of oak and pitch pine. The presence of oak provided food

Approximate shoreline at 8,000 yrs. B.P.

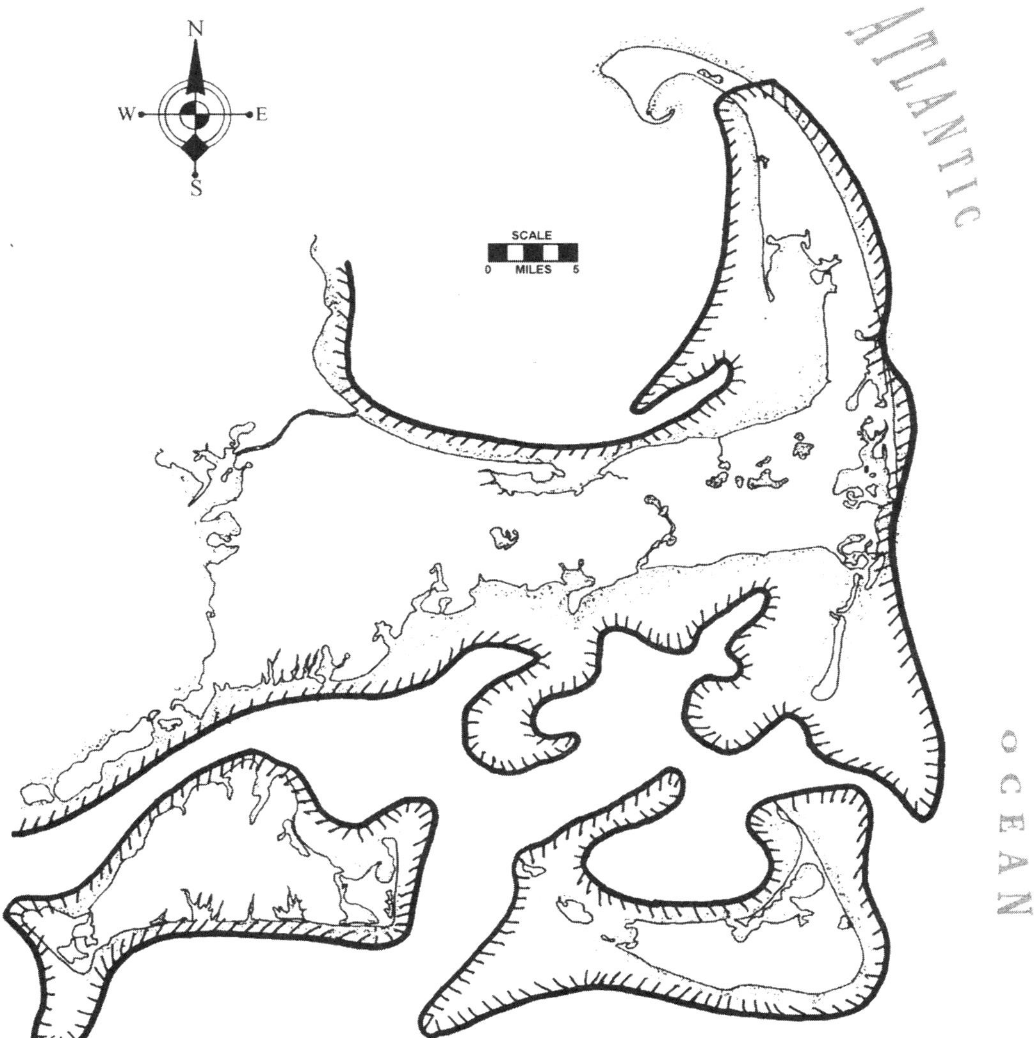

N
W · E
S

SCALE
0 MILES 5

ATLANTIC

OCEAN

B.P. = YEARS BEFORE PRESENT

Created with the assistance of:
Robert N. Oldale (U.S. Geological Survey) and Dr. Elazar Uchupi (Woods Hole Oceanographic Institution)

Map design by Water Mark Desktop Publishing – Eastham, Massachusetts

The photograph on the left shows two spear points—about 4,000 years old, found by Cleon Crowell in Brewster's Stony Brook Valley. These spear points were made during the Late Archaic Period, when seasonal settlements were established along the tidal rivers of Cape Cod.

The photograph on the right is of a large triangular spear point or knife blade found by Cleon Crowell at a plowed field in Brewster. This artifact was made during the Late Woodland Period when large settlements were located at the major bays and estuaries of Cape Cod. In addition to hunting, gathering and fishing, the people of the late Woodland Period were farmers who planted gardens of corn, beans, squash, and tobacco.

for white-tail deer, one of the most important resources for the Archaic Period population of Cape Cod.

Unlike the highly mobile Paleoindians, the Archaic Period population of southern New England, including Cape Cod, began settling down. The improving climate brought environmental change and a wide variety of seasonally available plant and animal resources to the region. Rather than moving the entire community across the landscape to resources, the native peoples of the Archaic Period settled seasonally in centrally located, residential camps from which hunting and collecting parties could operate. In the warmest months of the year, communities would be established near estuaries or wetlands which have since been submerged by the rising sea. During the period between the late fall to early spring, camps may have been established in the more protected interior uplands of Cape Cod, near sources of fresh water. More permanent settlements may have occurred as the population grew and the number of bands and territories increased, thus restricting the free movement of these communities.

Archaeological evidence collected from a number of sites at Herring River in Harwich, Bass River in Dennis and the Stony Brook Valley in Brewster clearly indicates that native peoples were living at least seasonally along the river valleys of the Cape by 9,000 years ago. Extensive settlements near the headwaters of these rivers attest to the importance of fishing at this time. Anadromous fish, like alewives, were seasonally abundant in these rivers. Other resources within the river valleys were also important. Edible plants, turtles, birds and both large and small mammals would have been sought by these hunter-gatherers. Between 1987 and 1990, members of the museum's archaeology program excavated a significant Middle Archaic Period site (6,000–8,000 years old) at Upper Mill Pond in Brewster's Stony Brook Valley. The excavation of that site is described in detail later.

In addition to the settling down that occurred during the Archaic Period, the type and number of material goods produced were greatly increased at this time. The native peoples of this period developed specialized tools for wood working—axes and adzes, and stone mortars and pestles for processing seeds and nuts. By 3,500 years ago, soapstone bowls for storage and cooking had been created. The presence of large soapstone bowls on Cape Cod during this time clearly indicates that native peoples here traveled west or south to find the raw material to make these bowls or traded for them. Because the seasonal camps were occupied by the same group or groups from year to year, these cumbersome implements could be stored at each camp.

The native peoples of the Archaic Period also developed a technology that allowed them to manipulate the landscape. The use of fire to create edges and clearings in a forest was used for the first time during the latter part of this period. The regular burning of forest

39

underbrush increased the density and productivity of certain plant species while establishing meadows or edges in the forest to attract deer and other animals. Native peoples could now control, to a degree, both the diversity and productivity of their environment.

The Archaic Period also saw the development of complex ritual systems involving cremation burials in which red ochre and a large number of stone tools were buried near the deceased. At one such site on Barley Neck in Orleans, more than 300 stone axes, adzes and blades were recovered from a single cremation feature. Archaeologists have long pondered the meaning of this complex ritual behavior.

By about 3,500 years ago, sea level rise had stabilized, and coastal processes began to define the modern coast of Cape Cod. Sediment eroded from marine scarps was carried by longshore currents that run parallel to the shoreline. As the sediments were redeposited, coastal barriers were formed. The developing barrier beaches provided protected embayments critical to the formation of the modern estuary systems. The estuaries and salt marshes that lay behind these beaches—The Great Marshes at Barnstable, Nauset Inlet and Pleasant Bay, for example—became the most productive environments on Cape Cod. By about 2,500 years ago, large communities were located at all of the major estuaries of the Cape.

CAPE COD IN THE WOODLAND PERIOD

The archaeological record clearly indicates that by the Early Woodland Period, the developing estuary systems provided resources for the native peoples of Cape Cod. It is important to note that native peoples undoubtedly sought and procured coastal resources prior to the development of the modern estuary systems, but the evidence of that activity has been lost as sea level has risen, drowning low-lying areas.

Collectors and archaeologists have found and excavated shell middens along the shores of Wellfleet Harbor, Nauset Inlet, Pleasant Bay and Sandy Neck. In a later chapter, we describe in detail the museum's excavation of an important shell midden at Pochet in the northern reaches of Pleasant Bay.

During the Woodland Period, the native peoples of Cape Cod pursued a wide variety of seasonally available resources—a pattern referred to by archaeologists as a *broad spectrum economy*. Native peoples of this period established large settlements along the shores of the bays and estuaries during the warm months of the year. During the winter months, the population broke up into smaller family groups which weathered the worst of the winter in protected hollows by freshwater ponds. While the plants and animals of the estuaries and salt marshes could have been collected at any time during the year, coastal

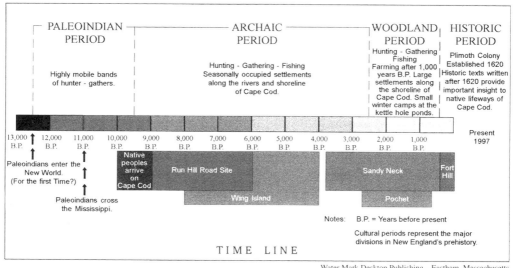

The chart above shows the major periods in the prehistory of the region and describes the lifeways of native peoples in each period.

resources like shellfish, tomcod, waterfowl seals and drift whales, would have been critical during the winter months when other foods were unavailable.

Archaeological evidence indicates that by 1200 AD the native peoples of Cape Cod had begun to farm, planting corn, beans, squash and tobacco. This development has been confirmed by two radiocarbon dates from Late Woodland shell middens at Pleasant Bay, recovered during museum excavations.

Trading with native peoples living to the south and west of the Cape brought copper, chert, corn, beans, squash and tobacco to the region. The production of clay pots gave Woodland peoples a means to prepare and cook both wild and domesticated plant foods.

A typical late Woodland community (1000 A.D.–1500 A.D.) might have consisted of several hundred people, with individual families tending their own small farmsteads within the village. Each year, sachems, or village elders, distributed land for garden plots. Planting areas were cleared and maintained by burning. Typically, gardens would be used for a season or two, then allowed to lie fallow.

Circular houses, made of bent saplings covered with mats of salt marsh grasses, were located next to the family garden. The houses were relocated as garden plots were abandoned.

Women and children gathered shellfish, nuts and berries, tended the gardens and maintained the household, while men hunted and fished. Each household produced food and materials for its own consumption, but by the end of the Late Woodland Period, there is evidence of surplus production, which would have been important for trade and the maintenance of political and social alliances.

By 1500 A.D., the native peoples of Cape Cod were, no doubt, marveling at the sight of European ships, unaware of the coming devastation. Within 200 years, the native peoples of Cape Cod would be decimated by disease and exploitation, and their lands taken, as the surging tide of European settlement swept across the Cape.

In the chapters to follow, we describe the museum's investigation of the culture and lifeways of the native peoples who occupied these shores before 1620. We detail the four major archaeological projects the museum has conducted since 1987. We review the purpose of each project, explain the field methods used and share what we learned.

This story is told by examining the inseparable relationship of cultural and natural processes that have defined both this landscape and the people who live upon it.

"The Cape is a mosaic of many kinds of patches of sand."
—ARTHUR N. STRAHLER, *A Geologist's View of Cape Cod*

Photo courtesy of Jane Booth Vollers

Geology for the Archaeologist:
A Primer

> With the ever-increasing flow of settlers and visitors to the Cape and
> Islands, there has been continuing speculation regarding the physical as-
> pects of these sandy lands; for they are in an endless state of flux, alive
> with changes measured not in geologic eons, as in the more static inlands,
> but within lifetimes, decades, or even overnights.
> —*These Fragile Outposts,* Barbara Blau Chamberlain

The history of Cape Cod is a narrative of continuous change, a rich tapestry woven from
the interplay of cultural and natural processes. The aims of geology and archaeology fit
nicely together on the Cape, a landscape "alive with changes," as Chamberlain calls it.
Here geologists explore the manner in which geological processes, such as sea level rise
and erosion, have shaped these fragile outposts, while archaeologists investigate how
these changes have molded the lives of the region's inhabitants.

In the course of every archaeological project at the Cape Cod Museum of Natural
History, we have turned to geologists, such as Robert Oldale of the U.S. Geological Survey
at the Woods Hole Oceanographic Institution, to help us reconstruct the ancient landscapes
that were once home to the native peoples of the Cape.

In the following pages, we offer a primer from geologist Oldale on the creation of
these sandy lands and on the geological processes that have given them definition.

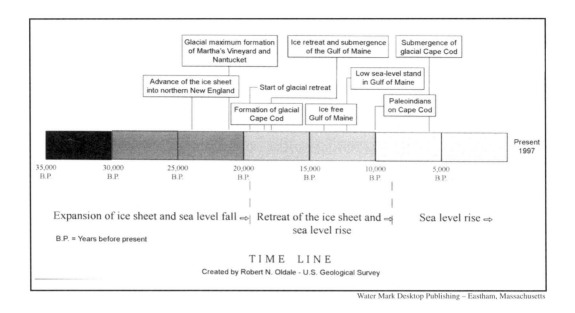

The chart above illustrates the major events in the geological formation of Cape Cod.

GEOLOGY OF THE REGION

> Far from being just a simple sandy peninsula, the Cape is a mosaic
> of many kinds of patches of ground, each different in origin from the patch
> next to it, but all fitted together by a single history of growth and change.
> —Arthur N. Strahler, *A Geologist's View Of Cape Cod*

Cape Cod owes its existence to a continental glacier and to the sea. Continental glaciers characterize the Pleistocene Epoch, the great ice age, that began about a million and a half years ago. Great masses of ice, called ice sheets, formed during glacial stages when the earth was cooler than it is today. The ice eventually melted as the earth gradually warmed. There have been so many glacial and interglacial (periods between glaciers) stages to date that this present geological epoch, the Holocene, may not mark the end of the ice age, but may only be a geological prelude to a glacial stage to come.

A glacial stage forms when the earth's climate cools and more snow falls during winter than can melt in summer. The snow accumulates layer upon layer, and the deeper layers compress to form ice. When the ice is thick enough to deform and flow, it becomes a glacier. The Laurentide ice sheet, the last of the great ice age glaciers in North America, began to form in Canada about 75,000 years ago at the beginning of the Wisconsinan Glacial Stage. About 25,000 years ago, it advanced southward into New England, and reached an area south of what is now the Cape and Islands about 21,000 years ago. Here, in a more temperate climate, the advance stopped, and retreat began when the glacier margin melted back northward faster than the southward flow of glacial ice.

As the glacier advanced, it scraped up soil and unconsolidated sediments, and gouged and plucked fragments of solid rock that lay beneath the ice. These materials were either carried forward in the base of the ice and deposited along the glacial margin to form moraines and kame and kettle terrains, or were carried by meltwater streams beyond the edge of the ice and deposited to form outwash plains. Three outwash plains—the Wellfleet Plain, the Truro Plain, and the Eastham Plain—characterize the glacial part of Cape Cod National Seashore. Glacial deposits that formed these outwash plains were laid down about 18,000 years ago by meltwater streams that drained from a glacial lobe that lay to the east of the Outer Cape.

At the close of the Wisconsinan Glacial Stage, the great continental glaciers retreated throughout the Northern Hemisphere, and water that was formerly trapped in the continental ice sheets, returned to the ocean basins causing the sea level to rise. As the post-glacial climate continued to warm, plants and animals that had been forced southward by the advancing ice began migrating northward. Evidence collected on the Cape suggests that by 13,000 years ago the region's vegetation consisted primarily of grasslands and coniferous woodlands (spruce). By 8,000 years ago, the forests on Cape Cod were a mix of coniferous and deciduous pitch pines and oak.

About 6,000 years ago, the rising sea reached the glacial deposits of Cape Cod. Waves eroded the loose glacial sand and gravel to form sea cliffs. Waves and currents transported and re-deposited this material to form beaches. Winds picked up the sand from the beaches and cliff faces and deposited it in the form of coastal sand dunes. Barrier beaches grew lengthwise, partly closing off embayments in the glacial landscape and forming lagoons protected from the open ocean. In these quiet shallow waters, salt marshes developed, as detailed in the chapter on Sandy Neck.

GLACIAL LANDFORMS

Most of the debris carried by a glacier is transported and deposited beyond the ice margin by streams carrying water away from the melting glacier. These layered deposits are called *outwash*. Meltwater flows through the crevasses of a glacier, and tunnels within and beneath the ice. As it flows, it gathers rock debris from the base of the ice and carries it to the ice front. Beyond the ice front, the meltwater forms glacial streams that eventually enter

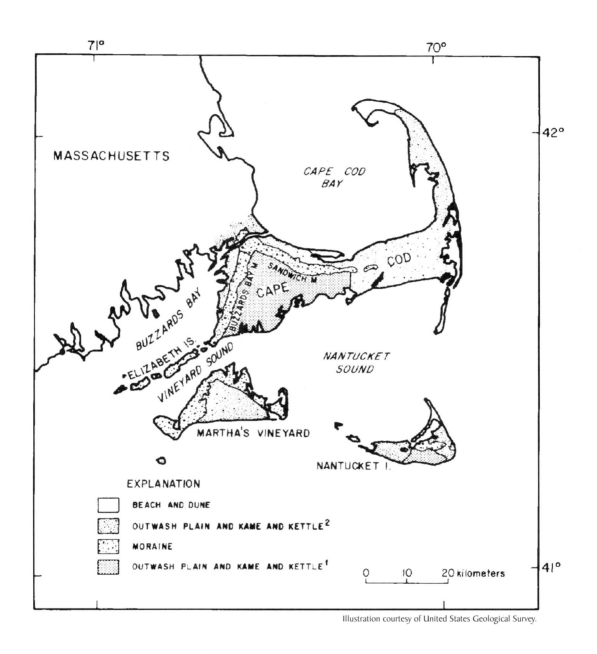

71° 70°

MASSACHUSETTS

CAPE COD
BAY

42°

CAPE COD

BUZZARDS BAY

SANDWICH M.

BUZZARDS BAY

CAPE

ELIZABETH IS.

VINEYARD SOUND

NANTUCKET
SOUND

MARTHA'S VINEYARD

NANTUCKET I.

EXPLANATION

BEACH AND DUNE

OUTWASH PLAIN AND KAME AND KETTLE^2

MORAINE

OUTWASH PLAIN AND KAME AND KETTLE^1

0   10   20 kilometers

41°

Illustration courtesy of United States Geological Survey.

Cape Cod owes its existence to a continental glacier and to the sea.

lakes or the sea. These streams transport rock fragments ranging in size from boulders to clay. Changes in the speed of the water flow sorts the debris, leaving behind fragments too large to carry. Generally, the streams flow fastest near the ice margin, and slow gradually with increasing distance from the margin. Thus, outwash is coarsest in the upper part of the outwash plain where it consists of large boulders and coarse gravel, and becomes progressively finer, grained downstream where it is mostly sand and gravel. When meltwater streams enter standing water such as lakes or the sea, the current slows rapidly and sand and gravel is deposited near the shore to form a delta. Finer particles, mostly silt and clay, are deposited on the lake bottom or sea floor.

The outwash plains of Eastham, Wellfleet, and Truro were formed this way. They are flat depositional surfaces that slope gently westward toward Cape Cod Bay, and were created by braided meltwater streams that drained from the South Channel lobe westward into what is now the bay. Outer Cape outwash plains are only remnants of the original landforms. During their formation, the upstream ends of the outwash plains were covered by the glacier. When the ice melted away, the surface collapsed and formed a hummocky area that sloped steeply toward the glacier. This feature is called an *ice-contact head*. There are few ice-contact heads of outwash preserved; many were overridden when the moraines were formed and others have been eroded by the sea. A preserved ice-contact head can be seen on the south side of Route 6A in the towns of Dennis and Brewster. The outwash plain surfaces are, in places, interrupted by holes that formed when large blocks of ice left behind by the retreating glacier and buried by outwash plain deposits melted away, causing the surface to collapse. These holes are called *kettles*. Many kettle holes are deep enough to reach the water table, and have become kettle ponds. Others, breached and drowned by the sea, formed salt ponds—a good example is Eastham's Salt Pond adjacent to the Cape Cod National Seashore Visitor Center off Route 6.

The large embayments of Nauset Marsh in Eastham and Pleasant Bay in Chatham, East Harwich and South Orleans are also glacial in origin. They represent sublobes of the South Channel lobe that extended farther westward than the main lobe. These lobes of ice prevented the deposit of outwash, and when the lobes melted, they left behind topographic lows. These low-lying areas became embayments when the Cape was drowned by the rising sea.

COASTAL LANDFORMS

The rising sea during the Holocene Epoch is the other major factor in the formation of Cape Cod. Sea cliffs or marine scarps are perhaps the most dramatic landform created by the erosion of the sea. Rising abruptly above the shore, sea cliffs in many places are more than

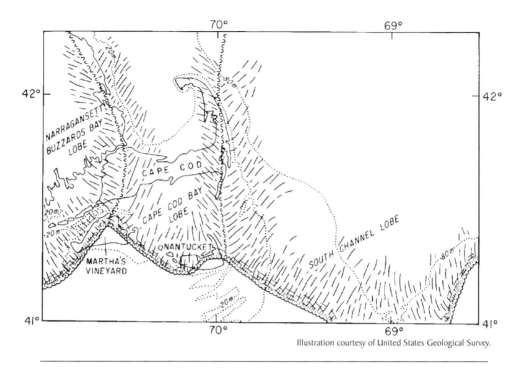

Illustration courtesy of United States Geological Survey.

The Lobes of the great glacier.

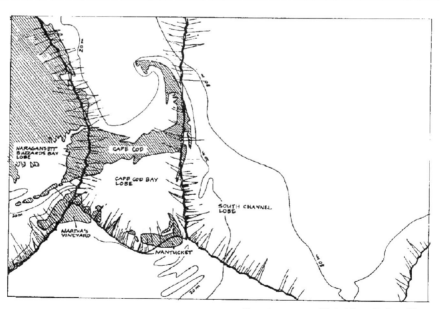

Illustration courtesy of United States Geological Survey.

Map showing the approximate limit of the Laurentide ice sheet, the glacial lobes, and the approximate location of the interlobate angles during ice retreat. Depth of ice below sea level (in meters) shown by thin lines.

100 feet (30meters) high, and reach heights of more than 150 feet (45 meters) along the eastern limit of the Wellfleet outwash plain between Newcomb Hollow and Cape Cod Light in Truro. The great cliff along the east side of the Outer Cape is more than 15 miles (24 kilometers) long, and would be an impenetrable barrier except for the hollows or valleys, such as Wellfleet's Newcomb Hollow and Longnook Hollow in Truro that interrupt it in places. Today, these hollows and others provide access to the beach for swimmers, windsurfers, and fishermen. In years past, they were the only way rescuers and salvagers could reach vessels stranded on the beach. The cliffs, at present, are exposed to the sea in most places, and are being eroded by large storm waves from fierce nor'easters. In a few places, the sea cliffs are separated from the ocean by beach and dune deposits that have been formed by progradation of the shoreline. These inactive sea cliffs, such as High Head in Truro, are usually covered by vegetation. Protection offered by the prograding beach and dune may be temporary; inactive cliffs could again be attacked by the sea.

Beaches on the Cape are formed when the waves transport sand from the nearshore to the shore and deposit it as narrow strands at the base of sea cliffs or as barrier spits across bays and estuaries. Waves transporting the sand rush up the beach obliquely. The water returns to the sea directly down the slope of the beach. In this way, sand grains are transported along the beach in saw-tooth path, a process called *longshore drift.* Sand is also transported along the shore by longshore currents, which are also generated by the approach of the waves. When an embayment in the coast is encountered, sand is transported into the embayment and deposited in the form of a *barrier spit.* Barrier spits, as we note in a later chapter, are generally long and narrow, and bordered by bays and salt marshes on their landward side. Spits are re-curved or hooked at their ends.

The hooking results from wave refraction around the end of the spit, which changes the direction of the longshore drift and, consequently, the shape of the spit. Good examples of re-curved spits include Race Point and Long Point in Provincetown, the south end of Nauset Beach in Chatham, and the south end of Monomoy Island.

Sand dunes constitute a major coastal landform on Cape Cod. In most places, the barrier spits are the foundation for the dunes. The sand on the beach is picked up by the winds and blown inland. During its passage inland, the wind slows and drops its load of sand to form dunes that cap the barrier beach. Dunes are shaped by prevailing winds and have gentle upwind slopes and steep downwind slopes. Sand grains are carried by these winds up the gentle windward slope, and deposited on the steep leeward slope. In this way, the dunes change shape and migrate. They also are shaped by the winds in other ways. On the Provincetown spit, there are U-shaped dunes with the open end facing the wind. These are called *parabolic dunes,* and they are formed when the wind blows away the sand at the middle of an existing dune, sometimes exposing the underlying beach deposits. The sand is dropped downwind along the advancing leeward face of the dune.

The most seaward dune atop barrier beaches parallels the shore and is called a *foredune*. During storms, the foredune acts to preserve the barrier island by protecting it from overwash. *Clifftop dunes* form a narrow band along the coast. Youthful unstabilized dunes are on the move as sand is transported by the prevailing wind. Older dunes become stabilized by vegetation including dune grass and forests. However, if they lose their protective vegetation, they will move again.

This process can be seen along Route 6 in Provincetown, where once stable dunes are advancing on the forest and highway and are filling in adjacent Pilgrim Lake.

BARRIER ISLANDS

Barrier spits, coastal dunes, sand and mud flats, and salt marshes make up a complex feature called a barrier island. *Barrier island* is a generic term that also includes barriers tied to a headland at one end, like most of the barrier islands on the Cape. The islands are elongate and bordered on one side by the sea and on the landward side by a bay or lagoon. Although longshore sediment transport and deposition are the major processes in the formation of barrier islands, other processes are essential in preventing the barrier island from being drowned by the rising sea. Storm waves wash over the island to carry beach and dune sand into the lagoon. Storms will breach the barrier island from time to time, and tides will carry sand into the lagoon to form a flood tidal delta. *Washover* and *tidal delta* deposits form a foundation for the barrier island and allow it to roll over itself, tank-tread fashion, to move landward into shallower water. Although these changes in the barrier beach are troubling to owners of shore property, they are essential to the mainte-nance of the barrier island. Without these changes, the barrier beach would eventually be destroyed.

OTHER LANDFORMS

Kettle lakes and ponds, common features on Cape Cod, owe their existence to the fresh groundwater that underlies the surface everywhere. The sandy glacial deposits are dry in the upper part and saturated with groundwater at depth. The upper surface of the satu-rated zone, called the water table, is at sea level along the shore and rises as the land surface rises. However, the rise in the water table is always less than the rise in the land surface so that the overlying unsaturated (dry) zone becomes thicker away from the shore. Kettle lakes and ponds form where the bottom of a kettle hole penetrates the unsaturated zone and enters the water table. Most kettle ponds and lakes have no inlet or outlet, but they are not stagnant. The water in the saturated zone flows through the glacial deposits toward the sea in the same manner that a stream flows to the sea, but at a much slower rate. This groundwater flow constantly refreshes the waters in the lakes and ponds.

Freshwater marshes and bogs, including those used to grow cranberries, form where the water table is at the surface or close to it. This can happen where the land surface is low or where organic and inorganic sediment have completely filled lakes or ponds. In these places plants adapted to wet soil can grow. Many freshwater marsh and bog deposits started to form thousands of years ago and some contain a nearly continuous record of the Cape's vegetation over the last 10,000 to 14,000 years.

THE FUTURE CAPE COD

The susceptibility of sandy Cape Cod to the forces of the sea is a strength, not a weakness. It ensures that the Cape will probably exist for generations in one form or another even if sea level continues to rise. Ultimately, the Cape may eventually be nothing more than islands of beach sand, capped by dunes and surrounded by sandy shoals, or it may be completely drowned like Stellwagen Bank to the north of Provincetown. But this won't happen for a long time.

In the chapters to follow you will see how the geological processes that created and shaped the Cape also provided both opportunity and constraint for the native peoples who, for more than 10,000 years, inhabited these sandy lands.

PART TWO

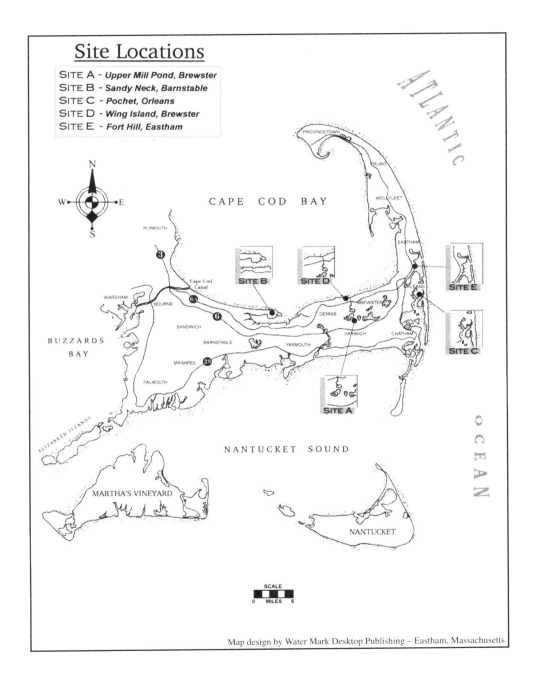

Site Locations

SITE A - *Upper Mill Pond, Brewster*
SITE B - *Sandy Neck, Barnstable*
SITE C - *Pochet, Orleans*
SITE D - *Wing Island, Brewster*
SITE E - *Fort Hill, Eastham*

ATLANTIC

CAPE COD BAY

PROVINCETOWN

TRURO

WELLFLEET

PLYMOUTH

EASTHAM

SITE B

SITE D

SITE E

Cape Cod
Canal

ORLEANS

WAREHAM

BOURNE

BREWSTER

DENNIS

SITE C

SANDWICH

HARWICH

CHATHAM

BUZZARDS
BAY

BARNSTABLE

YARMOUTH

MASHPEE

FALMOUTH

SITE A

OCEAN

ELIZABETH ISLANDS

NANTUCKET SOUND

MARTHA'S VINEYARD

NANTUCKET

SCALE

0   MILES   5

Map design by Water Mark Desktop Publishing – Eastham, Massachusetts

"I not only could see the event
or place in my mind's eye,
but could also hear it, and smell the wood fires."
—JOHN HANSON MITCHELL

Photo courtesy of Jane Booth Vollers

Light from a Distant Fire: 8,000 Years Ago at Upper Mill Pond

Certain familiar harbingers announced the arrival of summer in 1987: the green of the salt marsh was deepening; bluefish were running; the roads were hopelessly congested; and residents queued up anxiously for beach stickers. In mid-June, I began a season of archaeological fieldwork on the eastern shore of Upper Mill Pond, unaware that in the next 12 months archaeological knowledge of Brewster's Stony Brook Valley would be expanded by at least 8,000 years.

Upper Mill Pond is a classic kettle hole pond, formed about 19,000 years ago when a large block of ice, sloughed from the retreating glacier, became lodged in a sandy outwash plain. Over time, the ice melted, creating a large pond with exceptionally steep walls. Upper Mill Pond is the second of three connecting mill ponds whose clear fresh waters flow through the stone ladders of Brewster's Stony Brook herring run, down Paine's Creek and out into Cape Cod Bay.

In May and June, gulls stalk the brook, casting a shadow across the waters of the run, causing alewives, members of the herring family, to scatter to the banks of a seining pool. Responding each year to a biological clock at the strike of spring, thousands of alewives enter Paine's Creek from the bay to lay their eggs in the warmer fresh waters of the connected ponds, a phenomenon described by Brewster naturalist John Hay in his book, *The Run*.

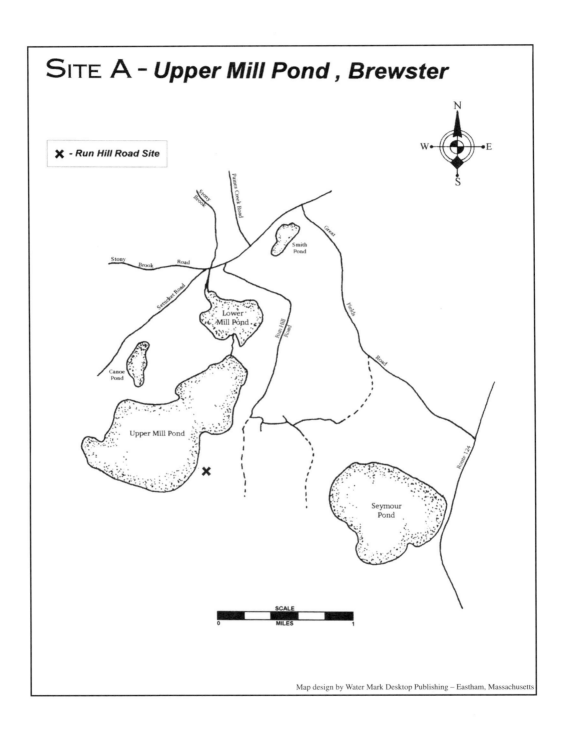

Site A - *Upper Mill Pond , Brewster*

✖ - *Run Hill Road Site*

Stony Brook

Paines Creek Road

Smith Pond

Great

Stony Brook Road

Schmucker Road

Lower Mill Pond

Run Hill Road

Fields

Canoe Pond

Road

Upper Mill Pond

Route 124

Seymour Pond

SCALE
0   MILES   1

Map design by Water Mark Desktop Publishing – Eastham, Massachusetts

Like salmon, these gray-green fish with silver sides swim upstream and actually leap up stone stairways to the mill ponds—Lower Mill Pond, Upper Mill Pond and Walker Pond.

Upper Mill Pond, the largest of the three, is surrounded by dense pitch pine and scrub oak trees. Today much of the land on the eastern shore is protected from development by town acquisitions between 1985 and 1987 which established an 835-acre forest of hiking trails called the Punkhorn Parklands.

DISCOVERY

Just outside the Punkhorn, there is a heavily wooded, two-acre bluff that offers a commanding view of Upper Mill Pond. The bluff rises about 50 feet above sea level. At the request of the property owner, Barbara Wallace, I visited the site in 1987. Wallace, then in her late seventies, had a passion for archaeology; she had planned to build on the property, but did not want to destroy an archaeological site if one were present. A member of the Cape Cod Chapter of the Massachusetts Archaeological Society, Wallace had participated in several local excavations. She was intrigued that her own property might contain a prehistoric site.

I had some knowledge of the area where Wallace planned to build. In 1984 on a one-acre parcel just south of her property, students on a museum-sponsored field trip had found several broken stone tools (mostly spear points) and large amounts of chipping debris (thin flakes of stone, the by-products from making stone tools). The land had been stripped of its topsoil, the "A" horizon, which exposed a layer of coarse, orange sand, called the "B" horizon.

To describe soil development in a given area, scientists use a sequence of lettered soil horizons, or layers. Leaf litter or humus lies on the surface of Cape soil. Below that is the "A" horizon, a dark brown-to-black soil high in organic matter. At the base of the "A" horizon, is a bone-white horizon where percolating water has leached the iron oxides out of the soil, depositing them in the "B" horizon below and forming an orange/brown rust stain on the coarse sand.

To a casual observer, the appearance of course orange sand on Cape Cod is not unusual. In fact, the Run Hill Road parcel looked like almost any other construction site on the Cape. But appearances are often deceiving, as they were in this case.

After obtaining permission from Wallace's neighbor in 1984, members of the museum's archaeology program had carefully searched the area south of the Wallace parcel, collecting artifacts from the exposed surface of the site. Additional chipping debris, as well as

Photo courtesy of Robert Oldale, U.S. Geological Survey

Typical profile of soil development on Cape Cod.

broken and unbroken stone tools, were recovered. We then completed a Massachusetts Historical Commission (MHC) site form to record the property on the state's inventory of prehistoric archaeological sites. The inventory provides archaeologists with a basic database that defines, in part, the distribution of archaeological sites within a given county. We called the area the "Run Hill Road Site." It was assigned the number 19 BN 592 (19 designates Massachusetts, BN abbreviates Barnstable County, and 592 is the number assigned to the site).

While we had successfully identified and recorded the site, we had little information about its size and no clear evidence of its age. When the bulldozer stripped the topsoil from the site, many of the stone tools were broken and randomly spread across the site, destroying its context—the place where the tools had been left, lost or discarded by the native peoples who occupied the site. As a result, we could not infer from collected artifacts what had happened at the site or when it had happened. The classic who, what, when, where and why questions could not be answered.

Driving to the site on a brilliant summer morning to meet with Wallace, I wondered what lay ahead. Had the Run Hill Road Site been completely destroyed, or did part of it lie, undisturbed beneath her property? When I reached the end of Run Hill Road, I turned onto a narrow dirt road that led through the pines to the top of the bluff. Wallace was seated in a lawn chair, a thermos of hot coffee by her side, binoculars in hand. She greeted me with many questions: How would I test the property? What did I expect to find? How long would it take?

As she inquired about the process, we walked the property. I kept my eyes to the ground, searching for artifacts. Within minutes, I found some chipping debris in loose sand in the road near my truck. I placed the tiny flakes of stone in a plastic bag and handed it to Wallace. We now had evidence that the Run Hill Road Site extended onto her land. With that question answered, we completed our plans for testing the property.

Two weeks later, I returned to Wallace's property with a truck full of shovels, trowels, screens, a compass, metric measuring tapes, camera, notebook and specimen bags— everything I needed to map and test the site.

Even though the site extended onto Wallace's land, finding subsurface artifacts and features, such as hearths and refuse pits, was not an easy proposition.

I spread a map of the area across the hood of my truck and studied it. Wallace's property was relatively small, about two acres, so I decided to excavate 50cm x 50cm shovel test pits at five meter intervals all across the top of the bluff. I thought I had a good chance of finding concentrations of artifacts and features by placing test units about 15 feet apart.

To create a grid of shovel test pits on the property, I placed wooden stakes five meters apart along the southern lot line. Using a compass, I laid out transects from these stakes to corresponding points on the northern lot line. I then walked along the transects (a straight line created by surveying equipment), placing flags at five meter intervals, marking each spot where I would excavate a test pit. By mid-morning, the top of the bluff was a colorful checkerboard of fluorescent orange flags, and I was ready to start excavating the shovel test pits.

Each test unit was carefully excavated in ten centimeter levels, a strategy that I hoped would allow me to determine the precise location of artifacts and features. I sifted each shovelful of dry coarse sand, using a box screen made from one-quarter inch wire mesh. In the very first test pit, I found several pieces of chipping debris. This pattern was repeated again and again as I continued north along the transect. Every test pit contained chipping debris, clear evidence that the Run Hill Road Site included a major portion of the Wallace property.

As time allowed, I worked at the project through August. Progress was slow because I was working alone. I spent most of my time excavating test units along a transect about 30 feet from the edge of the bluff. I was pleasantly surprised that every single test unit contained prehistoric artifacts. I was not authorized to test the property to the north, so I was unable to determine the precise extent of the site. Nonetheless, I spoke with officials at the Massachusetts Historical Commission and received permission to include the Wallace property within the area designated as the Run Hill Road Site. While I was excited by the prospects of developing new information about the site, it was clear that a tremendous amount of work lay ahead.

Most of the artifacts gathered from the test pits consisted of chipping debris. Only two identifiable stone tools were found: a broken drill and an unfinished projectile point, a general category referring to both spear and arrow points.

I was still unable to determine the age of the site because neither artifact was characteristic of a particular period in prehistory. Radiocarbon dating wasn't a possibility either. Given the acidity of the Cape's soils, organic materials, like nut husks or animal bones, were not preserved. Still, I knew we had made an important discovery. Systematic testing revealed the artifacts were not uniformly distributed across the site. While each test pit produced several pieces of chipping debris, one unit called T3-3 (transect 3, test unit 3) yielded more than 50 pieces—confirmation that the test pit had intercepted the main area where stone tools were made. I also knew the toolmaking area was relatively small because pits T3-4 and T3-2, located five meters east and west of T3-3, produced fewer than 20 pieces of chipping debris.

Only days remained in the '87 field season, and I was eager to continue exploring the site in hopes of recovering an artifact that would determine the age of the site. I decided to open two large excavation units next to T3-3. I needed help, so I called my friends Lenny Loparto, a colleague I had often worked with, and his wife, Barbara. I met Loparto, who is skilled in archaeological field methods, in the early 1980s when he hired me to work on an archaeological survey near Eagle Pond in Dennis. We quickly became friends, and often met to talk about our interest in archaeology.

Loparto and his wife were eager to assist me at Upper Mill Pond. On the last day of the '87 field season, we gathered at the site. In anticipation of a great "find," Barbara Wallace brought her family and friends.

In about an hour, we laid out two contiguous 1m x 2m units, one meter east of T3-3. We excavated these test units in 10-centimeter levels by a method called shovel scraping, using a flat shovel with a long handle to scrape, centimeters at a time, in an even manner across the floor of the excavation unit. Done properly, the shovel functions as an extension of the hand, much the way a trowel and brush are used when there is a visible stratigraphy within a site. Shovel scraping is an appropriate method of excavation when there is no discernible stratification—distinct, vertical layers of archaeological material defining the occupation history of a site. At Run Hill Road and at most other prehistoric sites on Cape Cod, archaeological deposits have been mixed or moved vertically by ants, earthworms, tree roots and, over the last few centuries, by the plow.

We screened the excavated soil through one-quarter inch mesh screens hung from tripods made from ten-foot two-by-fours. With three of us working, we were able to excavate the two units in about eight hours. As expected, hundreds of pieces of chipping debris were recovered, but to our disappointment, we were unable to locate a single stone tool that could determine the age of the site. While we all enjoyed the day, our failure to determine the age of the site was a disappointment.

The 1987 field season was brought to a close in September by my return to Amherst where I was studying for my doctorate at the University of Massachusetts. The next season's work, I decided, would focus on the area around T3-3. As I drove away from the Wallace property that day, I felt somewhat empty. We had the satisfaction of knowing we had identified an important archaeological site, and the frustration of not knowing what it meant.

During the winter, I analyzed the field notes and the artifacts we had recovered during the previous summer. Two things were apparent. First, all of the chipping debris was heavily patinated. *Patination,* or weathering, occurs to lithic (stone) artifacts that have been buried in the ground for long periods of time. The acidity of the soil causes the outer surface of the artifacts to fade in color as the stone is weathered. The chipping debris recovered from the Wallace portion of the Run Hill Road Site was weathered and seemed fairly old.

Secondly, the field notes clearly indicated that the majority of the artifacts were recovered from deep within the "B" horizon. When I had seen this pattern at other sites on the Cape, these sites proved to be thousands of years old.

EXCAVATION

The 1988 Field Season—have returned to site: located last year's N-S transect-T1: re-staked last year's STP's: located EU 1 and 2: laid out EU 3: will continue with 1 by 2 meter units through area of high artifact density.
—FIRST ENTRY IN 1988 FIELD JOURNAL

The 1988 field season began June 15 when I returned to the Wallace property on the eastern shore of Upper Mill Pond. As I had done at the end of the previous field season, I continued to explore the artifact concentration first identified by T3-3 by excavating contiguous 1m x 2m units (EU's).

These adjoining test units opened up a large area of the site and provided a broad, horizontal perspective, allowing me to map the locations of chipping debris and discarded stone tools. From the resulting pattern I could make inferences about what these ancient toolmakers had been doing. Recording this type of information was time-consuming. The center point of each stone tool had to be measured in centimeters from three points, the depth below ground surface, and from two perpendicular walls of a test unit, in essence pinpointing its location. While the work was slow, the payoff was almost immediate.

By noon of the second day, I had recovered the first diagnostic artifact of the project: a finely serrated projectile point undamaged from stem to mid-section, where it had been cleanly snapped. Although broken, the artifact placed the site firmly within the Middle Archaic Period, some 7,000 to 9,000 years ago (see illustration of projectile point). But even more important than the single artifact was its location within the site, its context. The point was recovered several centimeters above a concentration of reddened and cracked cobbles. A journal note provides the first description of that feature:

. . . now at 43 cm., and probably 40 cm., as level ended, noticed an increase in number of red "stained" felsite cobbles in definite association, brushed away surrounding soil and noticed pattern"
— DUNFORD, 6/16/88

What I had encountered were the remains of a prehistoric hearth or fireplace. The basin-shaped hearth, which had collapsed over time, consisted of about 30 cobbles occupying a space about 50cm x 50cm wide. The significance of such a feature was its

Photograph of the trowel and brush used to carefully expose the burned cobbles of the hearth.

potential for the recovery of charcoal or burned bone, materials that could be radiocarbon dated. Radiocarbon dating, if possible, would provide a much more accurate date for the occupation of the Run Hill Road Site.

By now, it was late in the day, and rain was threatening. The careful excavation and mapping of the hearth would take several hours, perhaps a full day. I decided to cover the hearth carefully so the walls of the excavation unit would not cave in during the rain. I then left for the night.

Early the next morning I returned to the site and developed a plan for excavating and recording the hearth. I removed the tarp and used my trowel and a small paint brush to carefully expose the burned cobbles. Unfortunately, because of the hearth's obvious age and the acidity of the soil only a few minute grains of charcoal remained—not enough for radiocarbon dating.

Using graph paper, I carefully mapped the hearth before removing the cobbles. The soil around the hearth was collected, and photographs of the feature were taken.

As I excavated the hearth, I recovered small amounts of chipping debris and a battered and burned hammer stone. This fist-sized cobble, discarded thousands of years ago as its edges began to crack and crumble, had at one time been an essential tool. Cobble hammers and antler batons and punches were the primary instruments used in the production and maintenance of stone tools, a process generally referred to as *flint knapping*.

At the end of the day, I began reviewing my field notes and the artifact inventory, a process that continued through the weekend. I was hoping to gain a better sense of the site. It seemed obvious that the hearth, or fireplace, was the focal point of this activity area. The highest artifact counts were recorded near the fireplace. I had recovered hundreds of pieces of chipping debris, a broken projectile point and a stone hammer. Interestingly, after a cursory examination it appeared that some of the pieces of chipping debris had been used as tools. As I inspected the edges of some of the flakes with a hand lens, I saw some evidence of use. In some instances, the edges showed polishing or micro-chipping, evidence that some of these flakes had been used as cutting tools.

Clearly more was happening here than the simple production of stone tools.

By early July, we had excavated four contiguous 1m x 2m units in the area surrounding the hearth. As indicated by this journal entry, an obvious pattern was emerging:

> . . .basically this unit [unit 4] followed a consistent trend - as we move away from FEA. 1 [the hearth] and the associated activity, the artifact density decreases..." —DUNFORD, 7/22/88

Throughout the summer, I systematically expanded the excavation area by linking 1m

Photo courtesy of Jane Booth Vollers

The photograph at the top shows the finely serrated spear point, snapped at mid-section, that was found just several centimeters above the hearth. This artifact is characteristic of the Middle Archaic Period and indicates that the Run Hill Road site is between 7–9,000 years old.

The photograph at the bottom shows the burned and battered stone hammer found within the hearth. This tool was used to break large flakes from cobbles found along the shore of the pond. The flakes were made into spear points such as pictured above.

Photo courtesy of Jane Booth Vollers

Photo courtesy of the Cape Cod Museum of Natural History

The photograph above shows the excavation area at the end of the 1988 Field Season. The area surrounding the hearth was opened up by linking 1 x 2 meter excavation units. A large box screen with 1/4" wire mesh hangs from a tripod. The backdirt from the excavation units was carefully sifted through this screen.

x 2m units north, south, east and west of the hearth. By now, I had established a consistent routine. Each day Barbara Wallace and I traveled to the site. Periodically, we were visited by Wallace's family and friends, who were fascinated by the project.

By the time the 1988 field season concluded in November, I had succeeded in excavating 14 contiguous 1m x 2m units, recovering 48 stone tools (most broken, discarded or unfinished) and 3,961 pieces of chipping debris. Significantly, 71 percent of the entire assemblage was recovered within a two-meter radius of the hearth. My observation, recorded in July, had been confirmed: the decrease in the density of artifacts beyond two meters was dramatic. Excavation unit 6, located three meters south of the hearth, yielded 54 pieces of chipping debris and no stone tools, while units 3 and 8, adjacent to the hearth, produced a combined total of 1,139 pieces of chipping debris and 6 tool fragments.

During my first week back at the museum, I inventoried artifacts that had been found that summer. Recovered stone tools included: fragments of stone spear points; cobble hammers; scrapers used in the preparation of wooden spear shafts or for butchering game; preforms (oval or teardrop shaped stone artifacts that represent a mid-stage in making spear points); triangular wedges of stone (produced from the radial fracture of larger stone blades) that were used to scribe wood or bone; and numerous pieces of chipping debris whose edges showed wear in the form of polishing, minute flaking or chipping (the sharp edges of chipping debris provided an expedient tool for scraping, scribing or cutting).

After creating the inventory, our attention turned to the processing and analyzing of the recovered artifacts. Each artifact was washed, then numbered with the site number and sequential catalogue numbers. For example, the first artifact, a preform fragment, numbered and prepared for analysis was 19 BN 592.1. A catalogue card was prepared for each artifact providing its provenience and details such as size, functional category, material, and use wear. Because we had obtained point provenience on the stone tools recovered during the excavation, we were able to re-fit many of the broken artifacts. For example, preform base "19 BN 592.1" re-fits with preform tip19 BN 592.2. These two artifacts were recovered more than five meters from one another. Analysis indicated that this preform was broken as it was being reduced to make a smaller spear point. Possibly these two fragments were thrown away in anger after they were accidentally broken.

After cataloguing the artifacts, I prepared a site map and examined the spatial distribution of artifacts surrounding the hearth. I also began to study the types of artifacts in the assemblage. It was clear that the site's occupants had been making and maintaining stone tools and that all stages of that process were represented in the assemblage.

In October of 1988, I attended the Massachusetts Archaeological Society's annual meeting in North Attleboro to present a paper offering a preliminary interpretation of the

Run Hill Road Site. The paper, *Workshops, Hunting Stands Or Huts,* explored the nature of the site area excavated in 1987 and 1988. Clearly, the production of stone tools was a significant, if not primary, activity at the Run Hill Road Site. Given this observation, I concluded that the concentration of chipping debris around the small hearth could have represented a "lithic reduction activity area," a prehistoric workshop where stone tools had been produced by a small number of individuals. Another possibility, indicated by the diversity of tools present in the assemblage, suggested the site could have been an area where people lived. The diversity of tools in an assemblage reflected a wide variety of activities other than simply making stone tools.

Yet a third scenario was suggested by the site's location. From the bluff high above the pond, the site's inhabitants would have had a panoramic view of Stony Brook Valley. Perhaps this was a hunting station where individuals waited patiently for game, passing long hours around a small fire as they prepared and maintained their tools?

Drafting the paper caused me to reflect more on what the Run Hill Road Site represented. More questions were raised then answered, but it was clear the Run Hill Road Site provided us with a rare opportunity to examine closely how stone tools had been made, maintained and used 8,000 years ago.

To assist me in this analysis, I asked a friend and colleague, Dr. John Cross, to join the project. Cross, an expert in lithic analysis (the study of stone tools), had just completed a doctoral dissertation on the subject.

In June 1990, John and I spent a week at the museum examining stone tools from the Run Hill Road Site. We both agreed that the internal consistency of the assemblage indicated a single occupation of short duration, thus allowing us to observe the technology of a given group of people at a specific point and place in time.

Weeks later, we returned to the site to excavate an additional ten 1m x 2m units. The results of that work confirmed previous observations. In September 1990, we backfilled the excavation area and assisted Barbara Wallace in planting a copper beech tree at the spot where we had excavated the hearth.

In all, we had excavated 24.5 contiguous 1m x 2m excavation units (a venerable old pine tree prevented us from completing one of the units). We had recovered 135 stone tools, and 6,842 pieces of chipping debris tabulated by level and unit, soil samples and a bucket of fire-cracked rock. We also had a three-ring binder with data recovery sheets for each test pit and excavation unit, a field journal, a stack of maps, plan views, profiles, photographs and slides, and catalogue cards.

But what did we have? What had we learned?

INTERPRETATION

For starters, we knew that some time during the Middle Archaic Period, 7,000 to 9,000 years ago, a small band of native people came to the eastern shore of Upper Mill Pond. Bands of hunter-gatherers like this were uniquely adapted to the mosaic of post-glacial environments that characterized southern New England and Cape Cod at that time. These bands moved frequently, finding and procuring resources as they became seasonally available. Indeed, their mobility was as much a tool as the finely flaked stone spears and knives they carried.

The environment then was much different than it is today. While sea level was rising, the shoreline was still some distance to the north and south of the Stony Brook Valley. Estuaries were developing where the shallow rivers and streams met Cape Cod Bay and Nantucket Sound. The climate was warmer and drier then, and the woodlands consisted of a mix of pine and oak species.

All in all, Cape Cod was a very attractive place for native people at that time. The estuaries at the shoreline and freshwater wetlands and ponds would have provided them with important resources. During warmer months, they may have camped along the shoreline, fishing, collecting shellfish and harvesting edible plants. In fall, winter and early spring, small groups of related families may have moved into the wooded interior of the Cape where they would have camped in sheltered valleys near freshwater ponds.

But who were the people who came to the eastern shore of Upper Mill Pond? Two different and yet plausible inferences can be made from artifacts recovered at the site.

One interpretation imagines a small group of hunters patiently stalking deer or other game in the valley on a cold fall day. Their families would have been several miles away at the winter camp. At the end of the day, the hunters have stopped to rest on the bluff above the pond. Here they had a sweeping view of the valley. They would have built a fire to warm themselves and begun to repair their hunting equipment. A broken spear point, snapped at mid-section, would be removed from its shaft, and replaced with a new blade made from one of the preforms carried by the hunters.

Members of the group gathered cobbles from the sandy bank at the edge of the pond. Stone hammers were used to break sharp flakes from the cobbles. Large flakes were made into scrapers or small spear points; other flakes were used to butcher the deer that had been killed that day. Early the next morning, the hunters moved on, leaving a smoldering fire, burned deer bones, some cordage that had been used to haft spear points to wooden spear shafts, broken stone tools and large amounts of chipping debris scattered in the sand around the hearth.

The artifacts found at Run Hill Road Site can be used to tell another story.

Perhaps the group that camped for a short time on the bluff above the pond was a family, traveling with other families from the winter camp to the shore of the bay where they would spend the summer. As the family rested by the fire, stone tools were made, a meal prepared and stories told. The group would have departed early the next morning, leaving a hearth filled with ashes and fish bones, several broken bone fish hooks, some cordage used as fishing line and broken stone tools and chipping debris. Thousands of years later only the hearth, stone tools and chipping debris remain.

Will we ever know which of these two interpretations is most accurate? Is there yet another story to spin?

My belief is that only time will tell.

"A long, lofty, wild and fantastical beach."

—REV. TIMOTHY DWIGHT

Sandy Neck:
Archaeology in the
Shifting Dunes

Sandy Neck is a classic barrier beach that stretches six miles east along Cape Cod Bay from the Sandwich-Barnstable town line toward Dennis. It is long and wide enough to have towering dunes and hollows that are graced with beach plums and wildflowers. Rare species of turtles and birds nest here. The long stretch of beach also protects the fertile Great Marshes behind, where small boats and canoes pick their way at high tide through narrow tidal creeks, framed by carpets of marsh grass.

In many ways, the history of Sandy Neck parallels the development of Chatham's old Monomoy, the elongated southern tip of Nauset Beach that has been broken into islands by the forces of the sea. "Sandy Neck is a prolongation of Spring Hill Beach, just as Monomoy is a prolongation of Nauset Beach, and it protects the old glacial shoreline of Barnstable in the same way that Nauset Beach protects the high shore of Eastham," historian Henry Kittredge wrote in his work, *Cape Cod: Its People and their History.*

> Though much older than Monomoy and generously sprinkled with patches of trees, it was formed in the same way from debris washed south and east from the bluffs of Manomet [at Plymouth]. Like Monomoy, it is growing longer by year, reaching out easterly across the entrance to the harbor toward the Dennis shore; whether or not it will ever reach this goal no one can say . . . Another thousand years will write the answer.

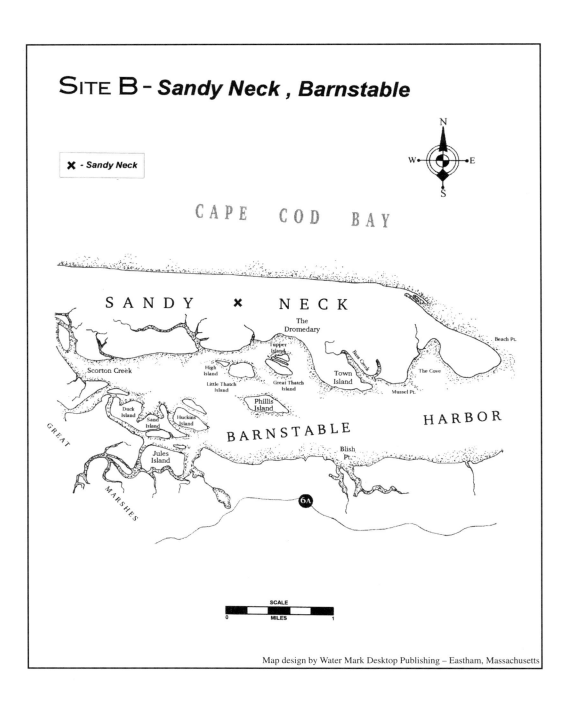

SITE B - *Sandy Neck , Barnstable*

✗ - *Sandy Neck*

N
W ● E
S

CAPE COD BAY

SANDY ✗ NECK

The Dromedary

Beach Pt.

Scorton Creek

Tupper Island

High Island

Little Thatch Island

Great Thatch Island

Bass Creek

Town Island

The Cove

Mussel Pt.

Phillis Island

Duck Island

Sand Island

Huckins Island

HARBOR

GREAT

BARNSTABLE

Jules Island

Blish Pt.

MARSHES

6A

SCALE
0   MILES   1

Map design by Water Mark Desktop Publishing – Eastham, Massachusetts

76

The Kittredge family has long ties to Sandy Neck. Jim Kittredge, Henry's son, continues to use the family cottage at the tip of the spit. I met him in the early 1980s when I first explored the archaeology of this haunting landscape. Searching for buried archaeological sites is always a difficult task, but on Sandy Neck, the search is complicated because the beach is always changing. The forces that shaped the neck—the prevailing northerly winds and harsh winter storms—alter the landscape with great frequency, exposing and burying archaeological sites.

Several decades ago, Dr. Lombard Carter Jones, a Falmouth physician and amateur archaeologist, was walking the neck one late fall afternoon when he saw a cache of prehistoric ceramic pots exposed high up in a dune. He decided to return there the following day to recover the pots, but that night a fierce nor'easter, with high winds, blew across the neck, leveling the dune and covering the pots, perhaps forever. The anecdote, published several years ago in *The Bulletin of the Massachusetts Archaeological Society*, captures both the transitory nature of Sandy Neck and the unpredictable manner in which archaeological sites on this beach are revealed and then hidden.

This chapter speaks to the difficulty of conducting archaeological research on such a dynamic, shifting landscape, a place far different than any I have ever explored.

OPENING DAY

The anticipation was great and expectations were high. I surveyed the barren, haunting landscape of Sandy Neck for a place to rest. It was mid-afternoon and the sun had begun its slow descent in the western sky. My partner, Doug Erickson, and I wrestled our packs to the ground as a transistor radio that we had brought along for company crackled in the crisp, quiet spring air. We listened for a moment. The contrast was striking. It was, after all, Opening Day, April 7, 1992. The Red Sox were the guests of Beantown's Nemesis, the New York Yankees, in a Bronx house that Ruth built. More than 280 miles away from the crowd and clutter, Doug and I sat quietly at the foot of the dunes on the lee side of the beach that Rev. Timothy Dwight in 1790 described as "a long, lofty, wild and fantastical beach, thrown into a thousand grotesque forms by the united force of the winds and waves."

We were here to conduct an archaeological survey of Sandy Neck for the Barnstable Historical Commission. The work was supported by a grant from the Peter F. Thorbahn Preservation Fund. Our job was to search every square foot of the neck, looking for exposed archaeological sites, like the one found by Dr. Jones years earlier.

The archaeological sites which lay beneath the dunes on Sandy Neck are in a precarious setting. When the dunes are re-shaped by nor'easters or winter storms, blow-outs (openings in the dunes) occur, exposing buried sites to both the elements and the prying hands of the curious. The resulting damage significantly reduces the archaeological value of the site. The artifacts are either disturbed or lost.

Before this project, the discovery of archaeological sites on Sandy Neck occurred by chance. The Barnstable Historical Commission in 1992 initiated the project to systematically search the neck early each spring for sites exposed by winter storms. The strategy was to locate and record archaeological sites shortly after their exposure, thus minimizing the damage caused by the elements or artifact collectors. The location of the sites were given to the Sandy Neck ranger staff who monitor the sites, checking for vandalism or further damage from erosion.

Erickson and I had spent most of "opening day," April 7 searching for sites deep in the dunes four miles out on the neck.

I first met Doug, a carpenter by trade, in 1991 when he asked for my help in recording a prehistoric site, eroding in a West Brewster sand pit. Erickson, a quiet man with a keen sense of humor, became a regular volunteer on museum archaeology projects.

The day's search had been for the most part unrewarding, and the Red Sox game was a pleasant diversion, as we waited for Jim Kittredge to drive us back to the parking lot at the entrance to the beach. Kittredge had volunteered to provide transportation around the neck during our ten days of surveying. When I traveled with Jim, he often talked of his grandfather—the late scholar George Lyman Kittredge—and of his grandfather's wonderful archaeological collection, much of which came from Sandy Neck. Kittredge drove an old flatbed truck with big tires, which when partially deflated cut through the loose sand of the beach with ease.

"Any news?" Kittredge asked with curiosity when he arrived in the top of the third inning.

"Yeah, Mo Vaughn just hit a home run," I replied in earnest.

"No, I mean did you see anything out there?" Kittredge asked.

"Not much today," I answered.

Unlike the Run Hill Road project, a major excavation, the focus of this project was to find and record new sites. Erickson and I searched the neck by foot looking for signs of erosion. We carefully examined each blow-out, looking for artifacts—stone tools, chipping debris, pottery, bottle fragments or any other indication of cultural activity. In some of these blow-outs, we found shell middens, campsites and bottle dumps. In each case, we measured the site with a 50-meter tape, photographed it, recorded observations in a field journal, and marked its locations on a map of the neck. Every site provided a glimpse into the past, allowing us to speculate about the lives of native peoples and the English colonists who walked this beach hundreds of years before us.

In the pages to follow, we review the growth and development of this dynamic barrier beach and salt marsh system over the last 4,000 years. We conclude by describing a typical day in the field, searching the dunes and hollows of Sandy Neck for clues to its past.

A WORK IN PROGRESS

Sandy Neck is a "work in progress." For the last 4,000 years, coastal processes have formed and shaped the barrier beach, while an extensive salt marsh system developed in the protected embayment behind the neck. By reconstructing the development of the beach and adjacent salt marsh. we can better understand the history and occupation of the neck by native peoples and English colonists.

The most distinctive feature of the neck, which is between a half mile and 200 feet wide, is its dynamic dune system. Some older, more stable, dunes along the southern margin of the neck are covered with pitch pine, white and black oak, tupelo, holly and sassafras. There is a little forest of native linden or basswood trees on the southern bank of a swampy hollow in an area of vegetated dunes about halfway down the neck. It was first described by botanist Henry Svenson, who also observed wild columbine (*Aquilegia canadensis*) growing within the hollow. Columbine, Sevenson speculated, grew on the acidic dunes because of the great quantities of shell from a prehistoric midden scattered throughout the hollow. That shell neutralized the acidity of the soil, allowing the columbine to thrive, Sevenson wrote.

The active primary dunes on the neck are adjacent to the open beach, and are partially vegetated either by grasses or by dense scrubby thickets of beach plum, poison ivy and bullbrier. Low, seasonally wet areas or swales between the dunes provide an important habitat for a variety of wildflowers. Other wetland habitats consist of abandoned cranberry bogs and cedar swamps. Aerial photographs taken between 1938 and 1991 record the development of an extensive pitch pine forest near the eastern end of Sandy Neck, and indicate its ecological diversity which attracted both native peoples and English colonists.

Post-glacial sea level rise has had the greatest effect on shaping the Cape's shoreline. Cape geologist Robert Oldale speculates that about 12,000 years ago, long after the glaciers had retreated far northward into what is now Canada, the sea was rising rapidly, perhaps 16 meters (or 50 feet) every 1,000 years. By about 8,000 years ago, Nantucket

This photograph of Sandy Neck provides an example of the active primary dunes, partially vegetated by dense scrubby thickets and beach grass.

Sound had been inundated and the low-lying area that would become Cape Cod Bay was almost completely submerged.

By about 4,000 years ago, sea level rise stabilized, and the Cape's arm-like shape began forming. Sediment eroding from marine scarps was carried by longshore currents running parallel to the shoreline. As the sediment was redeposited, coastal barriers were created. The developing barrier beaches, like Nauset Beach and Sandy Neck, provided protected embayments central to the formation of the modern estuary systems and salt marshes. Salt marshes constitute one of the most productive ecosystems in nature. Studies have suggested that a single acre of salt marsh can produce ten tons of plant material in a year. "Estuaries in general, and salt marshes in particular, are unusually productive places," note biologists John and Mildred Teal. "None of the common agriculture, except possibly rice and sugar cane production, comes close to producing as much potential animal food as do the salt marshes. The agricultural crops which approach this high figure are fertilized and cultivated at great expense. The marsh is fertilized and cultivated only by the tides."

FORMATION OF A SALT MARSH

The salt marshes of Sandy Neck grow today the same way they were formed thousands of years ago. The Great Marshes are as much a part of the neck as its dune system. The natural carving and shaping of this barrier continues, observes botanist Richard LeBlond, who describes the process in detail in this section from an essay in *A Guide to Nature on Cape Cod and the Islands:*

> The essence of the Cape brims in its salt marshes where most of the basic shoreline elements are present and interact: salt and fresh water; sand and tides; marine and terrestrial plants and animals. But land and sea do not merely meet here, they are in constant conflict. Beneath the visual serenity is a pitched battle of life and death, of destruction and creation, riding in and out with every tide. The salt marsh is a product of that battle and a prolific example of the ability of life not only to exist but to thrive in such a harsh habitat.

Despite these harsh conditions, writes LeBlond, the salt marsh is exceedingly productive. How can such a hostile environment produce so much life? We find answers by looking at the dynamic processes that form and maintain a salt marsh, but it can be summed up in one word: *adaptation.* LeBlond explains:

> Salt marshes form in quiet coastal waters protected from erosive wave action. The typical protector is a barrier sand spit, and the typical quiet water body is an estuary: a bay, harbor, or river mouth behind the sand

spit. On Sandy Neck, for example, the large barrier spit blocks waves from the bay, allowing the Great Marsh—the largest salt marsh on Cape Cod—to form behind its protective arm. Likewise, Nauset Marsh on the Orleans-Eastham line has built up behind the Nauset Spit barrier. Other examples include the marshland that has formed along the shore of the Martha's Vineyard Felix Neck Sanctuary behind State Beach on the coastal road from Oak Bluffs to Edgartown and the salt marsh behind Eel Point at the west end of Nantucket. Even small barrier spits will produce pockets of salt marsh as long as the waves are kept out and the tide is let in.

But wave protection and tidal influence alone will not establish a salt marsh, notes LeBlond. A suitable floor of sand is needed, one that is fairly flat and shallow to permit the growth of grasses that dominate, define, and nurture the marsh. The sand floor, known as *substrate*, is built up by a peculiarity of the tides. The rate of tidal flow into the estuary where a marsh forms is greater during the incoming tide than during the receding tide. In other words, the incoming tide has an ocean pushing it, while the outgoing tide is propelled only by gravity. The incoming flow is strong enough to carry sediment (mostly sand and silt) into the estuary, but the outgoing flow is not strong enough to carry the sediment back out.

This slow rise in the floor does two important things: it creates a habitat for the forming marsh and the continuous addition of sand allows the marsh to keep pace with a world-wide rise in sea levels. The stability that results from these processes is formidable, LeBlond says. The marsh deposits in the Great Marsh lying behind Sandy Neck reach a depth of at least 30 feet and represent four millennia of steady rise with the sea. It seems something of a miracle that one of the most dynamic and hostile environments in the world has created one of the most stable and uniform habitats.

DEVELOPMENT OF SANDY NECK AND THE GREAT MARSHES
Sandy Neck and the Great Marshes of Barnstable may be among the most intensely studied barrier beach and salt marsh systems in southeastern New England. Since the early 1950s, biologists have been drawn to the Great Marshes, where a significant record of sea level rise, beach formation, climatic and environmental change has been preserved within the salt marsh peat.

During the summers of 1952 and 1953, Patrick Butler, a graduate student in the Department of Biology at Harvard University, conducted field work at the Great Marshes as part of a research project on sea level rise and climate change. During the course of the field study, Butler took a series of cores at selected points across the widest part of the marsh. The purpose of the coring was twofold: to record the depth of the salt marsh peat to determine the rate of sea level rise during the last several years; and to recover pollen and

Photograph of the Great Marshes of Barnstable which lie behind Sandy Neck.
Salt marshes are one of the most productive ecosystems in nature. This salt
marsh system began to develop after 4000 years B.P.,
providing vital plant and animal resources to
the native peoples of the region.

spores preserved within the peat to reconstruct the vegetation history of the salt marsh and the surrounding environment.

In the summer of 1953, Butler took ten cores, the deepest of which was 29 feet. Preliminary results indicated that the marsh began forming about 5,000 years ago.

"Since the grasses forming the peat can only grow at rather restricted levels below mean high water," Butler concluded that there had been a gradual rise in sea level over the last 5,000 years. Unfortunately, Butler died the following year, leaving his study of the marsh unfinished.

But the potential of his database was obvious to his colleagues, Elso Barghoorn of Harvard University and Alfred Redfield of Harvard and Woods Hole Oceanographic Institution (WHOI). Redfield knew the significance of Sandy Neck and Butler's preliminary findings. He had spent much time on the neck. He was a close friend of Henry Kittredge and was a partner in the Mosquetucket Club, the Sandy Neck gunning camp that Kittredge and others had formed in 1908.

Barghoorn and Redfield completed Butler's study and published the results in 1959, a report confirming Butler's suggestion that the marsh began to develop several thousand years ago.

Redfield continued studying the Great Marshes in an effort to determine precisely how marsh systems were formed. In 1972, he published his findings in a study called, "Development of a New England Salt Marsh." The Great Marshes, Redfield wrote, "were well suited" for this type of study. He speculated that between 4,000 and 5,000 years ago, sea level had risen to the point where erosion west of the neck was dramatic. The longshore transport of sediment from west to east created a sand spit below Scorton Neck. About 3,000 years ago, this spit, now called Sandy Neck, began to assume its present form, and native peoples came here to sample the resources of the tidal flats and salt marsh.

Inside the spit, the salt marsh continued to develop in the protected environment of what was to become Barnstable Harbor. The processes of erosion, which were creating Sandy Neck, provided sediment for the development of sand flats inside the protected area. Bare sand flats, over time, were seeded naturally with *halophytes,* grasses that can grow within the intertidal zone (shallow tidal water). Redfield, in his report, described a pattern of succession in which the sand flats were colonized first by cord grass *(Spartina alterniflora),* then by salt meadow *(Spartina patens).* The natural cycle of sedimentation, colonization and succession, sea level rise and flooding led to the development of salt marsh peat. As the peat formed, the height of the marsh surface increased. This constant process of growth and decay provides the nutrients that make a salt marsh exceedingly productive.

As Sandy Neck developed and increased in length, more of the embayment inside the spit was protected, allowing for the continued development of the salt marsh. Concluded Redfield: "The clumps of grass become consolidated to form thatch islands and these in turn become joined to produce larger continuous areas of intertidal marsh and ultimately high marsh."

Today, the marsh is 3,170 years old, according to a series of radiocarbon-dated peat cores. "About 1,000 years were required for the sandspit to grow to one-half its present length, and an additional one thousand years were needed for it to extend to Mussel Point," Redfield wrote. "Beyond this point the growth of the spit in the past 1,200 years has been much slower, and most of the marsh is still in the intertidal stage."

ARCHAEOLOGY OF SANDY NECK

For generations, the exposed prehistoric shell middens and campsites of Sandy Neck have fascinated those fortunate enough to explore it. The diary of young Henry Kittredge, for example, describes his early adventures collecting artifacts on the beach. A July 7, 1903 entry, written when he was 13, observes, "But after a while we got over to Brailey's [sic] where we decided to land. Papa and I went ashore to look for arrowheads. We each found about seven."

The collecting journal of Cleon Crowell describes his exploration of Sandy Neck. One entry states, "Two fragments of pottery from Sandy Neck. I dug out with these one animal jaw with teeth, pieces of deer bones and other birds [sic] bones. The campsites were in the basins over among the sand dunes. Plenty of fish bones, big and small."

Other documents describe the use of Sandy Neck by English colonists after 1638. A land court document from 1935 describes the 17th century whaling industry on Sandy Neck: "It appears from the testimony of old witnesses that there had been in earlier days, a whaling house on the beach and the oil-soaked ground of a former try-yard on locus was still in evidence within the memory of some of the witnesses. . . The try-yard above referred to was near the house of Brayley Jenkins."

The fact that sites on Sandy Neck have drawn such attention during the last century is directly related to their accessibility. The dynamic nature of the coastal processes that created Sandy Neck often leave archaeological sites exposed, as noted in an excerpt from the unpublished field notes of archaeologist Edward Brooks:

> August 27, 1932: *Left F's camp in Bowser's canoe. A strong south-west wind was blowing, that kicked up a heavy chop. Arrived at Brayley's without incident and walked along the marsh for a quarter of a mile then cut in to the [shell] "heaps." Farther to the westward from where we had*

been digging on the previous days, was a high dune and along its base a thin blurred line that indicated a strata of shells. Digging in we found a strata about a foot in depth. F, who has roamed these dunes for forty odd years said that the strata was one he had never seen before. Further excavations disclosed that it stretched for some distance under the sands as well as into the dune that covered it.

Brooks spent portions of the next three years exploring the shell heaps and colonial sites in the immediate vicinity of Brayley Jenkins' property (see map). Shell heaps or middens, as noted earlier, are refuse deposits of varying sizes that consist primarily of marine shell, plant and animal remains, broken stone and bone tools, and discarded household items. The lime leaching from great quantities of shell serves neutralizes the acidity of the soil. As such, shell middens provide a wealth of information pertaining to prehistoric environments, resource availability, selection, procurement, diet, technology and settlement patterns.

Fortunately, Brooks was encouraged by Ripley Bullen of the Robert S. Peabody Museum of Archaeology to organize both his collection and field notes. Ultimately, with Bullen as senior author, Brooks' research was published in a 1948 *Massachusetts Archaeological Society Bulletin*. Bullen concluded that Sandy Neck had been occupied seasonally since prehistoric times:

> The present indications are that the exploitation of Sandy Neck by Indians occurred in relatively late, possibly pretohistoric, times (3000 years ago). History mentions the presence on Sandy Neck, at least in summer, of Indians whose usual abode was across the harbor at what is now called Cummaquid, a small settlement between the towns of Barnstable and Yarmouth Port.

Almost 20 years later, Bernard Powell explored Sandy Neck, identifying nine prehistoric stations. Powell's survey of Sandy Neck during the summer of 1965 confirmed the observations of Bullen and Brook about the location of shell midden sites on Sandy Neck. Wrote Powell: "Field observations substantiate and extend those of Bullen and Brooks (1948), who reported two concentrations of small shell deposits 'about two miles west' and 'about a mile and a half further west' from Sandy Neck Light, on the easternmost tip of the Neck."

While the exposed archaeological sites on Sandy Neck have stirred significant interest, most of the discoveries were not properly documented. The observations of people like Kittredge, Crowell, Brooks and Powell are particularly significant because their diaries, journals, field notes and published reports contained important descriptions of the archaeological record of Sandy Neck. As a result, archaeologists today can partially reconstruct the prehistory of Sandy Neck.

The photograph above shows a shell midden exposed by erosion on Sandy Neck.

The photograph below shows two spear points and a piece of pottery found by Cleon Crowell at Sandy Neck. The flake scars and edges of the two spears have been worn smooth by the blowing sand of the beach.

PREHISTORY OF SANDY NECK

It is clear from Redfield's history of the development of Sandy Neck that about 3,000 years ago the beach was a significant land form and an important place for native peoples, who used the neck to gain access to the resources of the developing estuary system—shellfish, fish, salt marsh grasses and waterfowl. In addition to the developing estuary system, the ecological diversity of the barrier beach also would have offered important plant and animal resources such as beach plums and other wild fruit, turtles and turtle eggs, and other animals. The native peoples of Mashpee used to gather beach plums on the neck every fall, bringing the harvest home by ox cart.

The generally exposed nature of the beach suggests that Sandy Neck may have been primarily occupied during the warmer months of the year. However, the neck may also have been visited during the winter by groups in search of seals, drift whales and shellfish. Some archaeologists have suggested that shellfish were a particularly important food source during the winter months. Perhaps, then, the location of prehistoric sites on the neck is related to the season of occupation. For example, winter sites might have been located within the protected hollows between the dunes, while summer sites were located near the open, eastern end of the beach. The majority of the known archaeological sites are middens.

None of the shell middens on Sandy Neck has been systematically excavated, but they contain evidence of domestic activities, such as the procurement and processing of a wide variety of plants and animals, and the production and maintenance of tools. This evidence confirms at least the seasonal occupation of Sandy Neck.

A BRIEF HISTORY OF SANDY NECK

While the prehistory of the neck is derived from the archaeological record, the history of Sandy Neck after 1620 is told primarily through historic documents. Over the centuries, there were many recorded events at Sandy Neck that chart its history and its transition from occupation by native peoples to the English ownership of the neck. Overuse, ultimately, threatened these resources.

A BRIEF CHRONOLOGY OF EVENTS

- In June of 1621, a small party left Plimoth Colony to search for John Billington, a boy lost in the woods south of Plimoth. William Bradford describes what the search party, traveling in a small open boat, saw as they approached Sandy Neck. This is perhaps the earliest description of the area surrounding Sandy Neck:

> We Anchored in the middeft of the Bay, where we were drie at a low water. In the morning we espied Savages reeking Lobsters, and sent our

Interpreters to speake with them, the channell being betweene them; where they told them what we were, and for what we were come, willing them not at all to feare us, for we would not hurt them. Their answere was, that the Boy was well, but he was at Nauset. . .

The search party was taken to meet Sachem Iyanough, the political leader of the community of Cummaquid at Mattacheeset on the shore of Barnstable Harbor. Bradford writes, "They brought us to their sachim [sic], or governor, whom they call Iyanough, a man not exceeding 26 years of age, but very personable, gentle, courteous and fair conditioned . . . His entertainment was answerable to his part, and his cheer plentiful and various." After dinner, Bradford and the others left for Nauset, with "Iyanough and two of his men accompanying us."

At Nauset, the Sachem Aspinet came to the search party and returned the boy. Bradford writes,

> After sunset, Aspinet came with a great train, and brought the boy with him, one bearing him through the water. He had not less than a hundred with him; the half whereof came to the shallop side unarmed with him; the other stood aloof with their bows and arrows. There he delivered us the boy, behung with beads, and made peace with us; we bestowing a knife on him, and likewise on another that first entertained the boy and brought him thither. So they departed from us.

The return of the lost boy provides insight into the political relationship of the community of Commaquid and Nauset in the early 17th century.

- In the fall of 1639, the English settlement of Mattacheese (Barnstable) began, and with it the European occupation of Sandy Neck. In 1641, Plimoth Colony granted permission to the small Mattacheese settlement to expand its vaguely defined boundaries, accelerating competition among the natives for the natural resources of the neck.

- On August 26, 1644, the "Serunk Purchase" was executed, granting to Mattacheese all of ". . . ye said lands and meddows lying betwixt ye bounds of Sandwich and ye bounds of Prexit another Indian . . .". This gave the proprietors control over most of the western half of Sandy Neck.

- On March 7, 1647, the Nepoyetum Purchase was signed, giving the proprietors legal possession of "lands on the north side between West Barnstable and the Yarmouth line." This parcel included the eastern half of Sandy Neck.

- Between the time of these two purchases until 1715, Sandy Neck was kept as common land for use by members of the community. The Great Marshes were held as "common lands" until their division in 1697 and 1698. During this period both the neck and the Great Marshes were intensively utilized. Salt hay was cut from the marsh and was used as fodder; the neck provided pasturage for livestock; and the whaling industry was established at Sandy Neck by 1651.

- The intensive use of Sandy Neck soon compromised the fragile ecosystem of the barrier beach. Deforestation and over-grazing led to erosion and threatened the very productive salt marsh system. In 1698, a law was enacted demanding that a fence be constructed at the western end of the neck to prevent livestock from gaining access to the beach.

- In 1711, the proprietors strengthened their efforts to prevent further erosion by requiring that: "every stranger both English and Indians that shall come and settle at Sandy Neck to goe on whaling voiages and not having interest themselves shall pay for their firewood, each person three shillings at entry." It is clear from this passage and the following one from *Proprietors Records, Town of Barnstable* that native peoples were still using Sandy Neck in the early 18th century.

- At a meeting in March of 1712, the proprietors were concerned with determining ". . . the best wale [way] of managing Sandy Neck and to make a report of what they shall doe at the next proprietors meeting." By 1715, the proprietors had developed a plan to divide the neck.

- The intensive use of the neck continued after 1715. In 1732, a measure was enacted banning all livestock from the neck except for the oxen teams used in the whaling industry. At the height of the inshore whaling industry (1725-1750), the neck had at least four try yards "where any citizen of the town who was engaged in whaling might erect a try-house and have room enough for his blubber barrels, lumber and other gear," wrote Henry Kittredge in *Cape Cod, Its People and their History.* A part of Sandy Neck is still called the 'Try Yard.'"

- In the 1800s, a cottage colony, with its own lighthouse and fishing fleet, was built at the western tip of the neck. Many descendants of the original occupants, Jim Kittredge included, still live there in summer. The colony can be seen from the docks of Barnstable Harbor.

1992 FIELD SEASON

A careful review of the archaeological record and history of Sandy Neck was essential to prepare for my 1992 survey of the neck. During the late fall of 1991 and winter of 1992, I poured over the research of Butler, Redfield, Brooks and Powell. I read all of the early historic accounts of the neck I could find, including Henry Kittredge's boyhood diary.

By March of 1992, I had received a permit from the Massachusetts Historical Commission to conduct the survey. Archaeological sites on Sandy Neck are protected by state law; for this reason, I am intentionally oblique about their locations.

The type of survey Doug Erickson and I conducted for the Barnstable Historical Commission is called a "walkover"—a search for visible archaeological sites. The location of the sites is recorded so that they can be studied and protected. After the survey was completed, our plan was to take aerial photographs of the neck to help us monitor the shifting of dunes and erosion of archaeological sites.

Our 10-working-days survey began in March 17. Due to inclement spring weather, the survey would not be concluded until the end of April. In many places, we found ancient dune surfaces, which appeared as thin black strands of sand that crossed the face of tall dunes. Some of these ancient dune surfaces contained prehistoric tree stumps. These "relict" dune surfaces were once vegetated and stable before being buried by blowing sands. On these surfaces, we searched for blowouts—places where wind or erosion had uncovered prehistoric artifacts or evidence of 17th century use of the neck by English colonists.

In some places, we discovered small amounts of chipping debris, stone tools and shell fragments dating back 1,000 to 3,000 years. In other places, we found "historic trash," fragments of glass, ceramics, and metal. Each time we came upon a blowout, we mapped it, photographed it and recorded all artifacts, as well as its location in relation to other features on the neck. This was exceptionally difficult. Often as we stood in a low-lying basins, our sight line to the horizon was obscured by the towering dunes that surrounded us, making it hard to chart where we were.

We discovered seven blowouts that spring; because our goal was to record the location of these sites, we spent little time collecting artifacts from the disturbed surfaces. In all, it was a successful survey.

Early in the afternoon on April 7, (the Red Sox opener, as noted earlier), a curious Erickson asked me as we finished mapping a blowout:

"Is this what you were looking for?"

Photo courtesy of Jane Booth Vollers

The photograph above shows a typical blowout in the dunes. We carefully searched blowouts like this for sites during our walkover survey.

The photograph below shows a shell midden exposed in a blowout. The top area of the photograph shows a thick layer of shell. The sand surrounding that layer of shell is black and almost greasy from the decomposition of plant and animal remains.

Photo courtesy of Jane Booth Vollers

This photograph shows a blowout in the dunes and a shell midden exposed by erosion. The midden appears as a heap of shells—hence the name shell heap used by Crowell and other early collectors. Ancient ground surfaces, buried by the dunes appear as thin, black strands on the face of the dunes.

An aerial view of the Neck, taken in the Spring of 1992. It is not possible to see blowouts from an airplane.

I told him that it was. Our survey had confirmed the research of Brooks, Powell and Crowell. Most of the blowouts were found in *swales* (basins) between the dunes, similar to where Crowell had discovered and recorded prehistoric campsites. I was disappointed, however, that many of these sites had been disturbed—all the more reason for greater protection.

With our walkover completed, we turned our attention to the task of photographing the neck by plane. In mid-April, Pat Anderson of the Barnstable Historical Commission arranged for a small plane to take us above the neck, and for photographer Steve Heaslip of *The Cape Cod Times* to take aerials. The task was impossible. We had to fly low enough to see the blowouts, and yet high enough for an accurate perspective. After a second attempt, we realized an alternative method was needed. The blowouts were simply too small to see from the plane.

At this writing, we are considering the potential of using satellite technology to map exposed sites on the neck, working closely with colleagues at the United States Geological Survey.

We are encouraged by this.

"Pochet is pronounced 'Pochey'...meaning to divide in two."
—WARREN SEARS NICKERSON, *THE BAY AS I SEE IT*

Pochet:
Archaeological Investigations at the Dividing Place

Early in the summer of 1991, I received word at the museum that a prehistoric shell midden had been exposed in East Orleans on Pochet Road, which meanders east across "Pochet Highland" towards the Atlantic. The midden was discovered on the southern slope of a prominent hill about 1,000 feet from Uncle Harvey's Pond, and less than a mile from the northern reaches of Pleasant Bay. The early occupants of Pochet drew great sustenance from the bay, whose shallow waters "ripple behind the low sand dunes of Nauset Beach," noted William Sargent in his journal, *Shallow Waters: A Year on Cape Cod's Pleasant Bay*. The bay, a 7,285-acre estuary system of tidal creeks, coves and salt marshes, developed over the last several thousand years in a protected embayment behind Nauset Beach. The beach, an 11-mile long barrier spit, stretches south from the sea cliffs at Coast Guard Beach in Eastham toward the shoals of Chatham's Monomoy Island.

During the summers of 1991 and 1992, I had a rare opportunity to explore the lives of the native peoples who occupied this sunny hillside at Pochet between 3,000 and 800 years ago.

AN ANCIENT LANGUAGE

Nauset. Mattacheesett. Pamet. Pochet. The names can be found on the street signs, shops and public buildings around Cape Cod. More than colloquialisms, these names are ves-

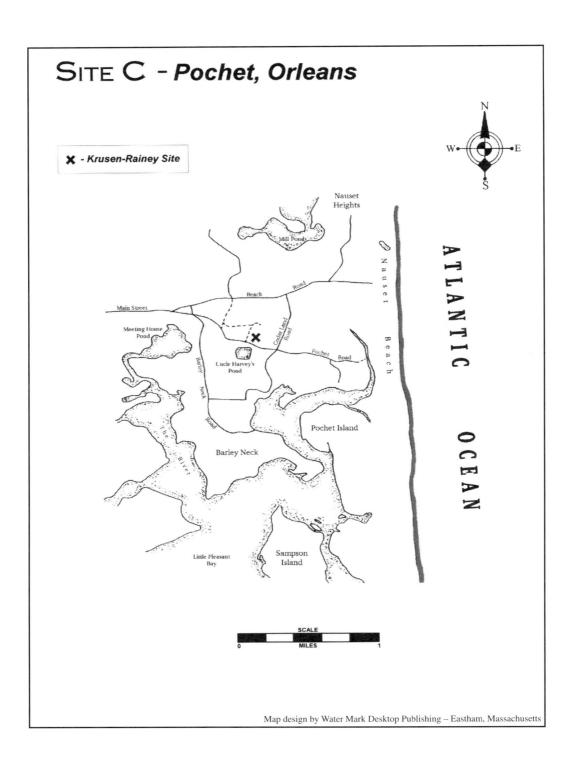

Site C - *Pochet, Orleans*

✗ - *Krusen-Rainey Site*

N
W E
S

Nauset
Heights

Mill Pond

Beach Road

Main Street

Meeting House
Pond

Uncle Harvey's
Pond

Barley Neck

Cohen Land Road

Pochet Road

Nauset Beach

ATLANTIC OCEAN

Road

The River

Pochet Island

Barley Neck

Little Pleasant
Bay

Sampson
Island

SCALE
0   MILES   1

Map design by Water Mark Desktop Publishing – Eastham, Massachusetts

98

tiges of an ancient and now extinct language—Massachusett, a dialect of the Eastern Algonquian language spoken by the native peoples of Cape Cod. These names and others have survived in the local vernacular because they refer to specific and meaningful places on the prehistoric landscape.

The meticulous research of historian Warren Sears Nickerson has kept alive many of these words that define the early environs of Pleasant Bay. "The beautiful tract around Round Cove [in East Harwich] and the West Shore, known to the Indians as Wequassett is again being called by its ancient name," Nickerson wrote in *The Bay As I See It*. "So is Monomesset, which we know as Great Point: Aska Onkton, the Indian Wading Place Path at the Head of The Bay; Pamuet where the Wading Place Path crossed the creek at the step stones."

Pleasant Bay, Nickerson wrote, was once "the Monomoyick Bay of the Indians, and Long Cove, or as it is sometimes called, Muddy River, was their Monomoyick River. Here, at the head of the Bay as it is locally known, was the tribal headquarters of the Monomoyicks. Their kitchen middens, scattered around the shores of Round Cove—the Wequassett of the Indians in East Harwich, south to the Wading Place, up the Monomoyick River and across to the waters of Ryder's Cove and Crow's Pond in Chathamport—hold skillfully wrought relics of their culture and blacken the soil where their wigwams stood."

Nickerson saw many of these relics, as did his friend and neighbor, Cleon Crowell, who spent hours exploring the wigwam sites and kitchen middens that line the shores of Pleasant Bay. Crowell was particularly interested in the pottery created by the native peoples of the Monomoyick and the Nawset communities. In his journal, Crowell noted the differences and similarities between potters of the two communities. "I have made a study of early Indian pottery" he wrote, "and my collection covers a wide range of styles and designs. The quality of pottery used by the Nauset Tribe was very much harder and firmer—a better grade so to speak than the grandchildren of chief Mattaquason used on the north bank of the Monomoyick River."

At the northern reaches of Pleasant Bay, there is a neck of high ground called Pochet or Pochet Highland which rises 50 feet above the sea. This pastoral jog of land divides Pleasant Bay from Nauset Inlet. According to Nickerson, Pochet is pronounced "Pochey" and is derived from the Massachusett word *Pohshe* or *Pahshe*, meaning to divide in two. Pochet, wrote Nickerson, was as much a territorial boundary as it was a geographic one, separating two distinct native communities. Literally, it was the "dividing line between the Nawsetts and the Monomoyicks."

> Those Indians who inhabited the Lower Cape on the arrival of the white man seem to fall naturally into three main groups, the Monomoyicks, the Nawsetts, and the Saquatuckets. While the dividing line between these

groups was not defined by metes and bounds, a Sachem's tribal domain apparently was recognized as taking in all of a certain drainage area, or watershed, and extending roughly to the height of land separating him from his neighboring Sachem's hunting ground. For instance: In the early days the height of the land in East Orleans known as Pochet was understood to be the dividing line between the Nawsetts and the Monomoyicks. North of Pochet Bay lay the Nawset Sachemry and the drainage area which flows into Town Cove and Nawset Harbor. The watershed on the south fed the headwaters of old Monomoyick Bay, now known as Pleasant Bay, around which lay the tribal lands of the Monomoyicks. The Sauquatuckets' lands lay west of the valley of Namskaket, which divided them from the Nawsets.

According to Nickerson, the highest ground at Pochet was the traditional division between two communities: the southern side of Pochet, where I excavated in 1991 and 1992, was occupied by members of the Monomoyick community; the north side of Pochet lay within the territory of Nawset.

Nickerson's observations of these ancient communities raises many questions. How important were the resources of Pleasant Bay and Nauset Inlet for these two communities? Was Pochet occupied seasonally? Was there a significant difference in the pottery made by these two communities, as Crowell noted? And if so, why? How formal was the boundary between the communities, and was it always in the same place?

In the summer of 1991, I explored these issues when a backhoe operator, in the process of installing a new septic system at a private home, struck a shell midden on the south side of Pochet Neck.

DISCOVERY

It had been more than 20 years since I had spoken with Jan Krusen, my fourth grade teacher at Harwich Elementary School. She called the museum late in May of 1991. Recent excavation work on her property had uncovered prehistoric artifacts.

"Would you be interested in taking a look?" she inquired. "I'm told it's a prehistoric shell midden."

I accepted the offer, and we settled on a date.

Days earlier, backhoe operator Don Williams, employed by the Paul S. Daniels Company of Orleans, had been excavating a trench for a new septic system at the Krusen property when he cut through the midden. Williams, who had uncovered many archaeological sites in his years as a heavy equipment operator, knew exactly what he had found.

Telltale black earth and crushed shell spilled from his bucket as he emptied the ancient debris onto the lawn next to the driveway. Immediately, he informed Krusen and co-owner Gail Rainey of his discovery, and the three then searched the backdirt pile for artifacts, filling a plastic container with prehistoric animal bones, chipping debris, ceramic sherds (pieces of pottery), and broken stone tools. Williams explained the significance of a shell midden to Krusen and Rainey. Anxious to learn more, they called the museum.

Shell middens are especially important because they preserve clues to prehistoric lifeways that otherwise would have decomposed in the Cape's acidic soil. In a shell midden, calcium carbonate (lime) leaches from the discarded shell as it decomposes, neutralizing the acidity of the soil and preserving organic matter such as bone, seeds and nut husks.

Middens, a term derived from the Danish word for kitchen, midden (*kjoekkenmoedding*) were central to domestic activity. Like our modern day dumps or landfills, these refuse piles grew over time as household garbage and other debris were discarded by a community. The great quantities of softshell clam, quahog, scallop, oyster and other species of shellfish in these middens offer clear evidence that shellfish were a staple in the diet of native peoples.

By studying shell middens, archaeologists can learn much about marine environments like Pleasant Bay and about the native peoples who lived on its shores. For instance:

- What foods were eaten by these people?
- How were meals prepared?
- Were clay pots used for cooking, storing food or holding water?
- How were stones and animal bones made into tools?
- How were these tools used?
- During what season or seasons was the midden created?
- Over how many years?
- How large was the community that created the midden?

Early in the morning on June 7, I threw my field bag containing a trowel, notebook, three-meter tape, camera and plastic bags into the back of my truck and headed east toward Pochet. I wasn't sure what I would find, but I was always eager to examine a midden.

As I turned into the Krusen driveway, I could see the two large pits that Williams had excavated. Backdirt piles, littered with shells and other debris, were just feet from the edge of the drive. Jan and Gail greeted me as I got out of the truck, and showed me to a small

Two views of the large pits excavated by the backhoe operator. Note the dark earth of the shell midden and the great quantities of shell littering the backdirt piles.

table along the side of the garage where they had carefully arranged the artifacts they collected: sliver-like fragments of deer bone; tiny fish vertebrae and fish scales; thin tubular pieces of bird bone, which I suspected were a species of waterfowl; about a dozen seals' teeth and piles of shell; whole quahog shells so well-preserved that they still retained the familiar purple coloration at the shell's edge; and a score of ceramic sherds. I was amazed at how well-preserved the animal bones were.

I then inspected the pottery in hopes of dating the midden. The discovery of pottery was helpful in determining the age of the site because pottery was not made on the Cape until about 2,800 years ago. I sorted the 20 sherds, each about the size of a quarter, into two piles. The first pile contained relatively thick sherds, about a centimeter thick in cross-section. The undecorated, smooth exterior of the sherds ranged in color from orange-brown to tan. None of the sherds showed evidence of carbon residue, sooting or any indication of burning that would have suggested the pots had been used for cooking.

The sherds in the second pile were thinner in cross-section and much darker. The exterior surfaces of some of these sherds were decorated. It appeared that a thin, perhaps comb-like, tool had been used to create parallel lines that ran across the surface near the collar or the mouth of the pots. The interior surface of many of these sherds had a thick, crusty, black carbon residue that indicated some of these pots had been used for cooking.

But the most distinguishing characteristic was the material that had been added to the clay paste to make the pots. Crushed quartz and granite were used in the clay paste of the lighter, undecorated sherds, while crushed shell had been added to the paste of the darker, decorated sherds. The additives, which archaeologists call *temper*, were used by the potters to enhance various physical properties of the vessels. The choice of temper was an important clue in determining the age of these vessels. On Cape Cod, shell temper was first used about a thousand years ago, while crushed quartz or granite temper was used much earlier when native peoples were first experimenting with this new technology. The two piles of sherds indicated the midden had been created between 2,800 years ago (the time of the first experimentation with pottery) and several centuries ago when shell-tempered clay pots were made by the native peoples of Cape Cod.

This was all I could tell about the site from the small collection of artifacts, animal bones and shell that were spread across the table. The real story was buried in the ground. I was anxious to look at the two pits Williams had excavated.

I went to my truck and took a trowel from my bag, then climbed down into the pit closest to the driveway. It was about a meter and a half deep, four meters wide and six meters long. By now the sun was high overhead and the temperature had climbed into the 80s. It had not rained in more than a week and clouds of dust kicked up around me as I

Photos courtesy of Jane Booth Vollers

Artifacts and animal bones found in the backdirt piles.

The photograph on the top left shows a shell-tempered ceramic sherd with a comb-like decoration on the collar of the vessel.
The photographs at the upper right and bottom left are animal bones:
those appearing in upper right are fragments of deer bone.
Lower left is a fragment of whale bone.
The photograph on the lower right shows grit-tempered pottery.
These are some of the first artifacts I saw
at the Krusen-Rainey site.

 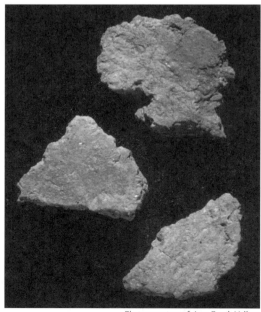

Photos courtesy of Jane Booth Vollers

worked, but I could clearly see sections of the undisturbed midden in the pit wall about a meter or so beneath the surface of the ground.

Krusen and Rainey stood on a backdirt pile near the edge of the pit and watched intently, occasionally asking questions. I scraped the edge of my trowel against the wall of the pit to expose a section of the midden, which was 10cm-40cm thick. In some places, I could actually distinguish between the individual piles of trash that made up the midden. The preservation was excellent. In the layers of the midden, I could see fragments of animal bone, charcoal and large pieces of pottery. I recorded this in my journal, and took several photographs.

While I was excited about the preservation of the midden, I was also puzzled. "Why was the site so deeply buried?" I wondered aloud. Krusen had an answer. About 30 years ago, several rooms had been added onto the house. To make room for the addition, a portion of the hillside had been leveled off and the fill had been spread across this part of the site.

By noon I had determined the midden was indeed worth testing. I climbed out of the pit and joined Krusen and Rainey, who were waiting in the shade by the garage.

"What do you think?" Krusen asked. "Do you want to excavate before we install our septic system?"

I was struck by the generous offer. "If you can give me about eight weeks, I can complete the testing," I replied.

We had a deal!

During the next two weeks, preparations were made to conduct a salvage excavation in the area that would be destroyed by the installation of the new septic system. Krusen and Rainey first had the old septic system pumped so it could be used in the interim, and received permission from the Town of Orleans to delay the installation of the new system until after Labor Day. I prepared a strategy to test the site and applied to the Office of the State Archaeologist at the Massachusetts Historical Commission in Boston for permission to excavate what I now referred to as the Krusen/Rainey Site. Given the urgency of the situation, the State Archaeologist quickly approved the permit, assigning it number 19 BN 657.

To secure funding for the project, I applied to the Friends of Pleasant Bay, a private non-profit organization that supported activities which both preserved the Bay and developed information about its natural and cultural history. The group was excited about the project and provided enough funding to allow me to hire a small team of archaeologists to help me with the excavation. Joining me were my good friend Dr. John Cross, who had assisted me at the Run Hill Road Site; Andy Sloan, who had also helped at Run Hill Road; and Doug Erickson, who I had recently met.

About two weeks before the crew was to begin work at the site, I encountered a problem. To excavate the area where the septic system would be installed, we would have to move much of the backdirt that lined the side of the driveway, a process that would take days to move by hand. The problem was solved when Williams stopped by for a visit late one afternoon while I was mapping the site.

"How are things going?" he shouted over the rumbling diesel engine of the 10-wheel dump truck parked near where I was working.

I climbed up onto the running board on the passenger side and explained the dilemma.

"No problem" he assured me.

With the blessing of his boss, Williams returned the following Saturday to remove the backdirt. The last hurdle had been cleared. By the end of June we were ready to begin. For the next six weeks, we worked long hours to reveal the layers of the midden that lay beneath this gently sloping hillside on the south side of the "dividing place."

EXCAVATION

During the first week of the field season, we created a grid across the site. To do this, we established a baseline oriented to 70 degrees east of north. Once we had done that we laid out the 10m x 10m grid, consisting of one-meter squares across the construction site. This checkerboard of one-meter squares allowed us precisely to map the location of the midden deposits, which had accumulated as individuals and households disposed of their trash and other debris. By studying the sections of the midden exposed in the pits Williams had excavated, I was able to determine that the occupants of the Krusen/Rainey Site had thrown their trash into a shallow depression. The history of the site and the story of its inhabitants would be told by reconstructing the manner in which the midden had accumulated over time.

Once the grid had been established, we excavated seven contiguous 1m x 1m excavation units in an L-shaped pattern to expose long north-south, east-west sections of the midden. To carefully map the midden deposits as they were revealed, each one meter square was sectioned into 50cm x 50 cm quads that were excavated separately.

Our strategy was designed to locate and isolate discrete deposits of refuse within the midden. In theory, each individual deposit represented a single moment in time. By carefully investigating these deposits, we would gain important insight into the daily lives of the site's inhabitants. Shell middens like this can provide evidence of other activities as well. Animals may have been cleaned and butchered on or near the midden. Potters may have

The top photograph shows contiguous 1 m x 1 m square excavation units arranged in an L-shaped pattern. Note that the midden is deeply buried. Planks and plywood were used to stabilize the dry sand of the excavation area as we worked.

The bottom photograph is a close view of the excavation of a 1m x 1m square excavation unit. The image shows the careful excavation by trowel of a 50 cm x 50 cm quad at the base of the midden.

107

come to the midden to collect aged shell for temper. They may have even burned sections of the midden to prepare the shell before they collected it. Latrine pits may have been dug into the midden.

Each 1m x 1m square was excavated by trowel, and the contents of the excavation units were screened through 1/8" wire mesh. The small mesh size allowed for the recovery of very fine objects such as seeds and fish scales, significant evidence for reconstructing both the local environment and the diet of the site's inhabitants. We also experimented with "wet screening," a process of using a fine spray to wash the backdirt from the excavation units through window screen. This process allows for the recovery of exceptionally small objects, like seeds. By recovering and studying seeds from the midden, we could tell what plants were collected and used by the people of Pochet.

We also had to develop a procedure for systematically sampling the shell that was recovered during the excavation, as we simply could not save all of the excavated shell. Due to the storage constraints of most museums and universities, archaeologists have explored a variety of procedures for retrieving meaningful samples of the shell recovered during midden excavations. We decided to save the shell from the northwest quad of each unit. In the other quads, the shell recovered in each stratigraphic level was weighed, and observations concerning the ratio of the shell species present were recorded. The shell was then discarded.

Within just a few days, this strategy began to reveal important details of the lives of the people who created this midden. In one excavation unit, we were able to isolate a deposit of scallop shell that was about the size of a bushel basket. The deposit was slightly mounded and contained large quantities of fish vertebrae and fish scales. The deposit was so well-preserved that some of the vertebrae were still connected! But most importantly, we discovered several burned kernels of corn within this pile of scallop shells. A radiocarbon date obtained from wood charcoal recovered from within the deposit told us that the scallop shells, fish bones and corn had been brought to the midden more than 700 years ago. This meant that by 1200 A.D., the native peoples of Cape Cod had begun to plant corn. Some archaeologists have suggested that the transition from hunting and gathering to farming was one of the most important events in the prehistory of the region. Others have argued that in New England, agriculture was only a supplement to hunting, gathering and fishing. This discovery placed the Krusen/Rainey site at the center of this important debate.

By the end of August we had completed the excavation of the seven units that we had laid out weeks earlier. While we had excavated only a very small section of the midden, we had developed some important information concerning the history of the site and the native peoples who created this midden.

This photograph shows a single deposit of scallop shell that was about the size of a bushel basket. The deposit was slightly mounded and contained fish vertebrae and scales, and burned corn kernels. Radiocarbon dating indicates that this deposit of refuse was thrown on the midden about 750 years ago.

The deepest levels of the midden contained thick, grit-tempered sherds similar to those found in the backdirt pile by Krusen, Rainey and Williams. Stone tools, specifically spear points, were also found in these levels. Both the pottery and stone spear points could be dated to about 2,800 years ago. Because this material was found in the deepest levels of the midden, at its base, we assumed that the site began to develop at that time. The presence of oyster shells and quahogs at this level indicated that Pleasant Bay had become a marine environment by at least 2,800 years ago. Interestingly, upper levels of the midden, which were created later, provided little evidence of the presence of oyster. This suggests that as the bay was developing, salinity levels increased and thus reduced oyster habitat.

Refuse deposits in the upper levels of the midden contained shell-tempered pottery and stone spear points that were made between 1,500 to 500 years ago. This would indicate that the midden was constructed between 2,800 to 500 years ago. The great quantities of stone tools and pottery from the later period suggest that the midden became increasingly significant over time.

During the last week of the project, we had long discussions with Krusen and Rainey about their plans for the site. We had completed testing the area where the septic system was to be installed in September, but there was a significant area of the site that we had not yet tested.

We also talked about what we had observed during the excavation. The site had great potential for addressing some significant archaeological questions. For example, the exceptional preservation of plant and animal remains within the midden would allow us to study how Pleasant Bay had developed over time. Our observation about the lack of oysters in the upper levels of the midden was a case in point. The remains of meals also could provide details about the diet of the native peoples who had created this midden; the presence of preserved corn within the midden was an exciting discovery. When did the native peoples of Cape Cod begin to plant corn and other vegetables such as squash and beans? And how did the transition to farming change their lives? The fact that we were able to distinguish between discrete deposits of refuse in the midden suggested that we could gain insight into the daily lives of the families and individuals who created these piles of shell. Krusen and Rainey, excited by the prospects, encouraged us to return to the site the following summer to continue our work.

During the summer of 1992, I returned to the Krusen/Rainey Site for an eight-week field season. In July and August, I worked with a crew of college students and adult volunteers to excavate an additional 17 1m x 1m units within the grid that we had built in 1991, bringing the total to 24 contiguous 1m x 1m units (see illustration). We followed the same procedures we had used during the previous field season, but with one exception:

Photo courtesy of Cape Cod Museum of Natural History

The top photograph shows the field crew working within the grid during the 1992 field season.

The bottom photograph shows a crew member using a brush and dustpan to expose individual deposits of trash within the midden.

Photo courtesy of Cape Cod Museum of Natural History

III

The top photograph shows the excavator placing the excavated material into a 5-gallon plastic bucket. Full buckets are lifted up and out of the excavation area and passed to other crew members who screen the buckets through box screens with 1/8" wire mesh.

The bottom photograph shows crew members searching a screen for artifacts.

The top photograph shows an individual deposit of quahog shell and fragments of deer bone at the base of the midden. The sign board shows the specific location of this deposit within the midden. The trowel is oriented to North.

The bottom photograph shows the profile of a pit at the base of the midden. Numerous features like this were discovered in the midden. They may have been used as latrines.

Photo courtesy of Barry Donahue, *Cape Codder*

An aerial view of the site taken at the conclusion of the project. This photograph gives perspective as to the extensive nature of the excavation

because of the excellent preservation of organic materials within the site, I had decided to rely more on wet screening in hopes of recovering small objects.

The results of the 1992 field season were consistent with the observations from our first year of work at the site. It was clear that about 2,800 years ago, a small group of people began living along this gentle slope, filling this hollow with their household trash and other debris. Greater numbers of people used this midden as time went on. But about 800 years ago, the midden ceased to be used, leaving us with perhaps the site's greatest mystery: why was the midden no longer important to the people of Pochet?

On August 28, we worked at the site for the last time. Before we backfilled the site, I wanted to make sure we had properly documented the area we had excavated. ComElectric, the local utility company, donated a bucket truck, and photographer Barry Donahue from *The Cape Codder* newspaper shot several roles of film from about 50 feet above the excavation area. At the end of the day, Jan and Gail and their family and friends joined us in celebrating the completion of the project. A week later, Williams returned to backfill the excavation area, using the same machine that had uncovered the midden two years earlier.

INTERPRETATION

Hundreds of hours of lab work follow every excavation. In this case, the lab analysis of artifacts, plant and animal remains necessary to interpret the Krusen-Rainey site continues. The Krusen/Rainey shell midden is a relatively small site that provides evidence of continuous seasonal occupation beginning about 3,000 years ago and continuing until about 1200 A.D. The location of the site, away from the shoreline, and its southern exposure suggest a winter occupation, possibly by a small group of related families. Late prehistoric period settlement patterns on the Cape suggest that after the corn harvest each year, large settlements located on the shores of the estuaries broke up into smaller family groups who spent winters in hollows around the kettlehole ponds. The Krusen/Rainey site is consistent with this observation. The analysis of fish bones, particularly the migratory species and the shellfish, will help us determine precisely when the site was occupied.

Since 1993, a small and dedicated group of volunteers has been working with my assistant Beth Nelson, sorting the shell recovered during the excavation of the midden. More than 120 sample units, some consisting of more than ten bags of shell, were collected during the two field seasons. Lab volunteers are working to sort the shell by species, part and size.

This tedious but critical task has several goals. First, we need to determine whether

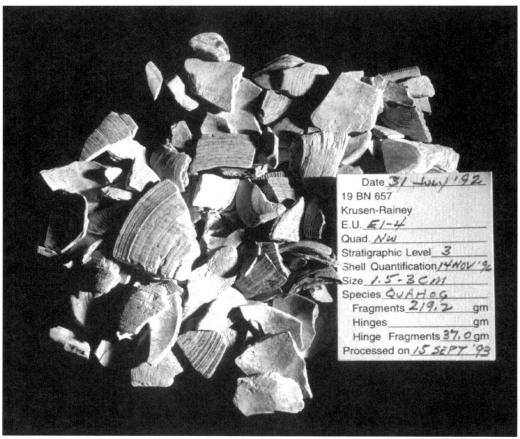

Date _31 JULY '92_
19 BN 657
Krusen-Rainey
E.U. _E1-4_
Quad. _NW_
Stratigraphic Level_ _3_
Shell Quantification_14 NOV '96_
Size _1.5-3 CM_
Species _QUAHOG_
  Fragments _219.2_ gm
  Hinges_____ gm
  Hinge Fragments_37.0_gm
Processed on _15 SEPT '93_

Shell fragments recovered during the excavation of the midden. They are being sorted and analyzed at the archaeology lab of the Cape Cod Museum of Natural History.

Photos courtesy of Jane Booth Vollers

The photo at the upper left shows two very small triangular stone arrow points found in the upper levels of the midden. Artifacts like this are thought to have been made between 1,000–400 years ago.

The photograph at the upper right shows two small arrow points found in the middle levels of the midden. Stone arrow points like this were made between 1,600 and 1,100 years ago.

The photograph at the bottom shows a stone spearpoint found in a refuse deposit at the bottom of the midden. Spear points like this were made between 3,000–2,500 years ago.

These artifacts found at the base, middle and top of the midden provide a general chronology for the occupation of Pochet and the formation of the midden.

Photo courtesy of Jane Booth Vollers

there was a change in the type of shellfish consumed over time. As noted earlier, the lower levels of the midden contained significant deposits of oyster shell, but oyster is not very common in the upper levels of the midden. Was this the result of environmental change as suggested or cultural practice, or both? We are also interested in mapping patterns of crushed shell within the midden. Did the potters here deliberately crush and burn shell for temper, and is this evident in the samples returned to the museum's lab?

The shell-sorting project is a good example of the many types of information-gathering that are associated with the excavation of a midden. But it takes time and a significant amount of patience to complete the task.

I can picture that sunny hillside at Pochet a thousand winters ago. Several *wetus,* small circular houses made of a framework of bent saplings covered with mats of salt marsh grasses, are nestled snugly between the pine trees. Wisps of smoke curl from the smoke hole in the roof of each *wetu.* Baskets of shellfish are stored in a nearby snowbank. A deer carcass hangs from a tree as the meat is aged; it is kept high enough so dogs cannot reach it. Firewood and kindling are piled in a clearing between the houses. In one of the *wetus,* a mother and her two children are grinding dried corn from the summer's harvest, using a stone mortar and pestle. In another house, a grandmother uses a bone needle and cord-age made from plant fibers to stitch two beaver hides together. The warm fur blanket is for a new grandchild.

Old men sit on a pine log in the sun, and share a pipe and stories of the past, while boys set snares in the woods near the top of the hill, hoping to catch rabbits or other small game. Several men are cleaning fish at the edge of the shell midden. They throw the skin and bones of the tomcod, or frostfish caught on last tide, onto the midden.

This indeed was a special place—home to small groups of people, perhaps related families, who weathered the worst of winter in this sunny hollow protected from the cold north wind. From the nearby woods and waters of the pond and bay, the people of Pochet could harvest everything they needed to sustain themselves during the long winter months.

Pochet was a place people occupied for thousands of years, and it must have become part of the legends, stories, and history of those who called it Pohshe.

"It may be surprising to hear that in nature nothing is finally known." —JOHN HAY

Solving the Mysteries
of Wing Island

Wing Island is a 140-acre preserve of heavily wooded upland in West Brewster that rises from a high salt marsh just north of the Cape Cod Museum of Natural History. The marsh is thick with salt meadow hay, spike grass, bulrushes, black grass and seaside goldenrod. Named after Brewster's first English settler John Wing, the island is owned by the Town of Brewster, and the museum maintains a well-traveled one-mile trail that leads across the island out to Cape Cod Bay, past patches of highbush blueberry, chokeberry, sea lavender, beach plum, wild raspberries and arrowwood, whose long straight shoots were once used by native peoples to fashion spears and arrows.

Wing, a disaffected Sandwich Quaker, purchased the land in 1656 from Edward Bangs of the Mayflower Company. According to one version of local history, Wing lived on the island with his family, but there is no proof yet of this.

For years, I had taken this land, literally in the museum's backyard, for granted, assured that town by-laws and conservation sanctions would keep the secrets of the island safe. It wasn't until 1994—12 years after I had joined the museum as staff archeologist—that I seriously considered the archaeology of Wing Island. I was encouraged in this work by museum co-founder John Hay.

"Solving The Mysteries Of Wing Island" is a story of discovery and of the painstaking process of gathering and interpreting clues to the past. To my surprise, Wing Island has yielded artifacts as old as 8,000 years, near the time when native peoples first occupied

Cape Cod. Artifacts discovered here are as old as those found at the nearby Run Hill Road Site, inviting speculation that the people who occupied Wing Island once camped at Upper Mill Pond. Excavations in years to come are sure to yield additional surprises.

DISCOVERY

Late in the fall of 1994, I called John Hay to discuss future projects. Hay had been instrumental in establishing the museum's archaeology program. During our conversation, Hay told me that while exploring Wing Island the previous month, he had found some old bottle glass, fragments of ceramic plates, pieces of metal and other bits of household debris scattered across a heavily overgrown area. Hay's curiosity was piqued because these remains, found in a remote spot on the western side of the island, appeared to date back to the 19th century. Neither of us knew of any residential use of the island during the latter part of the last century. Eager to enjoy one more day in the field before the onset of winter, and intrigued by what Hay had discovered, I agreed to explore the island with him.

And so with great anticipation on one of the last fine days of autumn, we headed down the Wing Trail, crossing the marsh on a narrow wooden boardwalk that rests upon an old causeway connecting the mainland to the island. The marsh is bounded by Paine's Creek to the east and Quivet Creek to the west, both brackish tidal creeks that empty into the bay. From here, Wing Island appears as a knob of land from across the marsh, framed by scrub oaks and pitch pines. At the head of the path, there is a wooden sign that notes some of the island's history and its ties to old Brewster families.

We walked on. Hay stopped to peer deep into the thick tangle of brush that framed the trail, seeking any familiar landmark that would lead us to the site. After 20 minutes, we found it. About 30 feet off the western side of the path, in a thicket of honeysuckle, we could see pieces of broken glass, ceramic sherds, fragments of enamel pots and what appeared to be pieces of porcelain. In any other season, these artifacts would have been hidden from view by the foliage of this dense vegetation.

We bulled our way through the brush, entered a relatively small clearing beneath several large oak and pine trees, and began to pick through the sherds and broken pieces of glass. It became obvious that we were not the first to find this site. The area had been disturbed years earlier, perhaps during the 1960s and 1970s when bottle collecting was a popular past time. The material was strewn about shallow depressions and backdirt piles. I looked for bottle fragments, specifically neck and lip sherds to examine the mold seam to assess the age of the bottles. After 1903, most bottles were machine manufactured, with

SITE D - *Wing Island , Brewster*

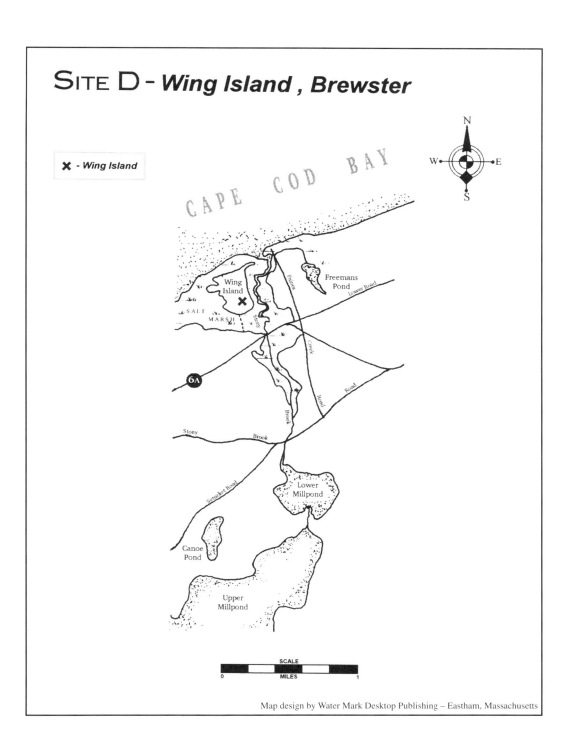

✖ - Wing Island

CAPE COD BAY

N
W · · E
S

Wing Island
✖

Freemans Pond

Lower Road

SALT MARSH

Stony

Paines

Creek

6A

Road

Road

Brook

Stony   Brook

Setucket Road

Lower Millpond

Canoe Pond

Upper Millpond

SCALE
0   MILES   1

Map design by Water Mark Desktop Publishing – Eastham, Massachusetts

123

An aerial view of Wing Island.

the mold seam extending from the base all the way to the top. There are other characteristics that can be used to determine age. For example, up until about 1860, bottles were free-blown and show the presence of a pontil scar on the bottom of the bottle where the glass was snapped from the blow pipe.

The majority of the bottle fragments we found suggested the site dated back to just before the turn of the century. The variety of bottle and ceramic ware indicated a residential use. While the discovery was of minor significance, a site not at all uncommon on Cape Cod, it provided an important catalyst for the museum's study of Wing Island.

As Hay and I left that area to continue on toward the bay, we raised many questions. Did John Wing really live on this island during the seventeenth century? Who created the small bottle dump Hay had discovered? What might remain beneath the ground of the extensive salt works that covered the western half of the island? What about the prehistoric occupation of the island? How old was the salt marsh?

Perhaps the most thought-provoking question came from Hay himself.

"How come we haven't surveyed the island yet?" he asked.

I had no answer.

By late afternoon we had completed our trek across the island and returned to the museum. Hay left for home, and I went to see museum director Susan Lindquist to talk about our walk.

"We know *very* little about the island," I told her. "Maybe it's time to start thinking about conducting an archaeological survey of the island."

The seed had been planted.

I left Lindquist's office unaware that our discussion had defined the archaeological work of the museum well into the 21st century. I spoke to Hay over the weekend about conducting a survey of the island. He supported the concept, as did Lindquist when we met again.

And so I began to gather information about the Island's history. In the museum's library, I found a worn manila file folder that contained useful information about the town's acquisition of the island in 1961, including a surveyor's map which showed the location of cement boundary markers.

After I reviewed everything I could find at the museum, I decided to visit Janine Perry, a Brewster historian and author. Perry is knowledgeable about historical patterns of land use on Cape Cod. She showed me a copy of an 1868 United States Coastal Geodetic Survey map of the Brewster shoreline. In numerous places along the shoreline, black and white checkerboard symbols indicated the location of saltworks. The entire northwest corner of Wing Island was dotted with these symbols. But the map also provided a surprise—

the location of the causeway that Hay and I had assumed had been built in the early 1900s.

Perry pulled another survey map of the island from her desk. Drawn in 1908, it was a revision of the 1868 map. It showed the saltworks—wooden vats once used to extract salt from seawater using an evaporation process—but the causeway was missing. Apparently, the heavy earthen causeway had sunk into the spongy peat of the marsh. It was rebuilt years later. The oldtimer had been right.

In addition to resolving the question of the causeway, we talked about another mystery of Wing Island: Did Wing and his family live there in the mid-1600s? We both agreed that when Wing and his family left Sandwich to settle in Brewster in 1656, he most likely traveled in a small open boat, similar to the shallop used by Plimoth colonists. The family may have landed on the north shore of the island, somewhere between Quivet and Paine's creeks.

While all this was speculation, Perry was able to document certain historical details about the Wing family, Wing Island and their role in Brewster's history. Perry provided me with a history she had written of Wing's arrival in the Stony Brook Valley.

HISTORY OF WING ISLAND

Wing, Perry writes, was the first English settler of Brewster. In 1659, he reportedly settled on land on the west side of the Paine's Creek-Stony Brook Valley. Of course, in 1659, this area was not within the bounds of any township. In local folklore, Wing is labeled a squatter, probably a myth that originated in the following entry in the Plymouth Colony records on March 1, 1659:

> The court, taking notice that John Wing is erecting a building in a place which is out of the bounds of any township . . . do order that the said John Wing . . . shall be prohibited to persist therein until it be cleared to what township such lands belong on which they build.

But this was not a case of trespassing. To the ruling fathers, settlements had to be orderly: that is, first determine where taxes are owed, then plant the homestead. And so, two months later a court order directed all persons on the west side of the Satucket River (Paine's Creek-Stony Brook) to pay taxes to Yarmouth.

At 44, Wing—the father of five children, a freeman of the colony, a jury man, and a first settler of Sandwich—was entitled to a share in the common lands. This is not the profile of a squatter.

The 1868 U.S. Coastal Geodetic Survey Map that shows the Brewster shoreline. The checkerboard-like symbols show the various places where saltworks were located.

So why did he come here?

Wing and his brothers were Quakers, and in the late 1650s, Quakers in Sandwich were punished by fines and disenfranchisement. In Sandwich, they were forced to endure the repeated pestering of a constable named Barlow, who enforced the colony laws against Quakers with a zeal. Wing's move to this area may have represented a search for stability, peace of mind and above all a good arm's length from the turmoil in Sandwich. His Quaker friend, John Dillingham of Sandwich, followed him just a few years later.

But Wing's move may also have been motivated by a desire to improve his estate in life. The area was rich in resources. The island and surrounding Stony Brook Valley had everything that a 17th century man of the soil was seeking: ample salt meadow for live-stock fodder, a ready source of fresh water, a strong tidal flow for a mill, woodland for fuel, a herring fishery, and most importantly, proximity to the bay for communication, transport, trade and, if necessary, for escape.

Wing and Dillingham purchased their land, which ran from the island to Nantucket Sound, from men known as the Purchasers. Several of the founding members of the Ply-mouth Colony had bought the patent to the colony from the London merchants who had financed the colony venture. In 1641, these Purchasers turned that patent over to the free-men of the colony, and, in return, reserved three tracts of land for themselves. One of these tracts was bounded on the west by what is now the Dennis town line and stretched to the east of Namskaket, a river on the Brewster-Orleans border. The tract was bounded on the north by the bay and on the south by Nantucket Sound. In 1653, the Purchasers made their first land division in the reserved tract and divided the northwest corner into 11 lots. By 1666, after a flurry of 17th century land conveyancing, Wing, Dillingham, Kenelm Winslow, Andrew Clark and Paul Sears had each acquired several of these lots for their homesteads. They set about extinguishing all ownership rights of the Purchasers to the area west of the Stony Brook River, now known as Paine's Creek, from sea to sea. They joined together in a Propriety, a form of common ownership and joint administration of land, and called them-selves the Setucket Proprietors, owners of land from Bound Brook, now Quivet Creek, to Stony Brook and "from sea to sea"—an area today encompassing all of Brewster and parts of Dennis and Harwich.

But the Purchasers were not the rightful owners of the land. There were Native Ameri-can proprietors of this land—the most important of whom were the Saquatuckets.

What we know of the 17th century native peoples of Wing Island and the Paine's Creek-Stony Brook Valley, we know through the paper trail left by the Setucket proprietors in their efforts to rid the propriety of Native American claims. The area of their first settle-ment in northwest Brewster was claimed by the heirs of a Barnstable sachem, Napaoitan, who brought a protest against Wing before the Colony Court in 1675 for "his detaining wrongfully a parcel of (their) land whereupon he hath built, fenced and otherwise improved."

Wing managed to settle the dispute in 1676 by paying the heirs ten pounds and four shillings.

The area from the mill ponds, at the present day grist mill on Stony Brook Road, south to Nantucket Sound belonged to Saquatucket sachem, Sachemas. On February 18, 1690, Sachemas gave Wing the deed for all of the land bounded on the east by a line running from the Stony Brook Mill dam south to Nantucket Sound; on the south by the sound; on the west by the Herring River and Napaoitan's land; and on the north by a line running through the ponds to the beginning at the mill dam. The purchase price was seven pounds.

Thus, by 1690, the Setucket Proprietors, having settled all outstanding claims against this territory, gathered from time to time to make orderly dispositions of their land, lay out roads and settle any disputes in their propriety. In 1694, these proprietors, including Wing, joined with proprietors of land east of Stony Brook and successfully petitioned the General Court for incorporation as a township. By 1739, the last of the common lands in the propriety had been divided. Parcels were set aside for a school, a watering place at Canoe Pond, and access to the herring fishery at Stony Brook Mill site.

The original proprietors of the Paine's Creek-Stony Brook Valley, the native peoples, had lost forever control over these lands. With a great appreciation now of the history of Wing Island, my goal was to tell the story of the island from its first occupation by native peoples to the present.

1995 FIELD SEASON

By late January 1995, I had spent many weeks gathering information about Wing Island. Everything I reviewed—historical accounts, newspaper reports, maps, books, and photographs—placed Wing Island at the center of local history. Paine's *History of Harwich* clearly described the manner in which Wing acquired the island. An 1868 coastal geodetic survey map used a checkerboard-like symbol to show the location of the saltworks covering the northwestern corner of the island. That same map showed an ancient way leading from the mill at Stony Brook to the causeway which crossed the marsh, linking the island to an important center of early commerce.

I also reviewed my notes concerning archaeological sites in the area. The proximity of the island to the Run Hill Road site and the fields from which Rennie, Crowell and others had collected suggested to me that the island must have been occupied by native peoples thousands of years before the arrival of Wing. But while everything hinted at the island's archaeological importance, we still had no material evidence of its long history, and we had to overcome some considerable natural obstacles.

During the last 60 years, the island has gone through a natural succession from an open field environment to a thick tangle of honeysuckle, poison ivy and bullbrier which grows between the scrub oak, pitch pine and red cedar trees. This thick vegetation now obscured the sandy surface of the island, keeping evidence of past use and occupation hidden from view. As with the earlier survey done at Run Hill Road, locating subsurface sites on the island would be a difficult mission. In addition to dealing with the thick vegetation, our strategy for testing had to take into account our limited budget and a short annual field season. It now became clear that this survey would take years to complete.

Early in the spring of 1995, I began the task of developing a research design and methodology for testing the island. I decided the most efficient way to survey the island was to map a single north-south transect across it. From that baseline, transects running east and west could be established. Shovel test pits, similar to those dug at Run Hill Road, would then be excavated at five-meter intervals along the transects; I assumed that a five-meter interval gave us the best probability of finding buried evidence of any past activity or occupation of the island.

By April, I had developed an elaborate plan to support our archaeological investigation of the island. I then sent the research design and methodology to the Massachusetts Historical Commission for approval. I also sent copies to Brewster's Town Administrator Charlie Sumner and the Conservation Commission. In addition, I also attended several public hearings, describing in detail, for the various regulatory agencies, the full scope and duration of the project.

By May, with the proper permits in hand, we were ready to begin the process of preparing a map for the field season. Mapping the island would be difficult. I had to find a registered bound or some other permanent fixture on the landscape to use as a datum point to anchor the baseline.

I needed a surveyor. One of my co-workers at the museum, publicist Anne Painter, was engaged to Peter Lajoie, whose family owns Felco Engineering in Orleans. Lajoie was eager to contribute. Late one afternoon in May, I met Peter in my office at the museum, and we studied an early plan of the island drawn in 1926 which had been found in the drawer of an old wooden map case in the museum's library. I was hopeful one of the cement boundary markers on the plan could be used as a datum point for the project.

Pictured above, Peter LaJoie sets up the surveying instrument on the island.

Pictured below are the locations of the stations and transects that were established during the 1995 Field Season.

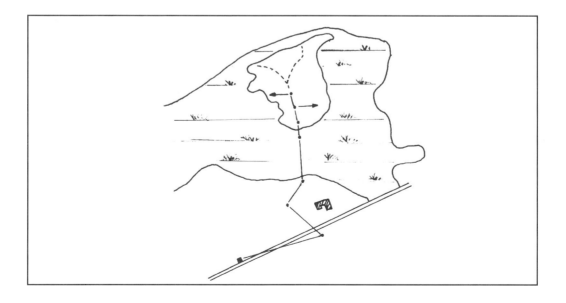

We spread the map out on a table so Lajoie could study it carefully. Although the cement bounds on the island were tied to one another (lines on the plan had been drawn between the bounds, indicating the distance in feet and inches between each point), the bounds were not connected to any reference point on the mainland. From a surveyor's perspective, the island was floating in space. The cement bounds on Wing Island were useless to us. We would have to develop our own map.

During evenings after work in June, we created a map, using surveying equipment provided by Felco Engineering, to tie points on the island to points on the mainland. The map would be used to plot the distribution of artifacts recovered during the testing of the island. The spatial relationship of the artifacts—the pieces of the puzzle—would essentially tell us the story of Wing Island.

But first we needed to find two established reference points on the mainland to begin the job of mapping the island. Lajoie suggested using two Massachusetts highway bounds located on Route 6A. He had a map indicating highway markers a short distance from the museum parking lot. After a brief search, we found the first granite highway bound in thick brush on the north side Route 6A. It was buried under three inches of sand. We now had a starting point. Our plan was to locate and map the island from these reference points on Route 6A. Once on the island, we would establish a series of points, or stations, from which all of our transects (straight lines running north/south and east/west) would originate. Each transect and every shovel test pit would then be tied to known points on the mainland.

The surveying instrument we used is called a *Total Station*. It records distances and angles using an infrared beam shot from the surveying instrument to a prism attached to a metal rod. We used the Total Station, commonly called the "gun," to create a series of straight lines from the highway bounds out to the island. Once on the island, we plotted a series of stations, or points about 30 meters apart, along the narrow cartway that leads to the bay. Each station was marked with an oak stake and given a letter designation, starting with A. From Station C and Station D, we created east/west running transects that would be the focus of our work during the summer of 1995. We also created a station in the small field just east of the path, thinking it would be a good place to begin the project. By the end of June, our surveying work was completed. Now the project could begin in earnest.

Early on the morning of July 10, a muggy summer day, 14 eager students and volunteers crowded into our newly-renovated archaeology lab. For the next six weeks, this small workspace would be the staging area for testing the island.

I spoke to the group about our strategy, which was to excavate shovel test pits at five-meter intervals on transects laid out from points established during the surveying work. Each line would be laid out using a compass and a 50-meter tape. Because we would

Photo courtesy of Cape Cod Museum of Natural History

The photograph at the top shows crew members excavating a shovel test pit in the field on the first day of the project.

The photograph at the bottom shows project assistant, Beth Nelson, assisting crew members in identifying artifacts.

Photo courtesy of Cape Cod Museum of Natural History

have to cut through the dense vegetation that covered most of the island, it was impossible to predict how long our investigation would take.

I divided the crew into teams of two. One team member would excavate shovel test pits, while the other carefully screened the backdirt through a box screen made with quarter-inch wire mesh, recovering artifacts and recording information concerning what was found and its location within the test pit. Each team was given a shovel, screen and a five-gallon plastic bucket containing trowels, metric tapes, plastic bags, marking pens, pencils, rulers, five-meter tapes, and a clipboard with field forms. I spent the first few hours reviewing various procedures to be used in excavating and recording each test pit. The group was small enough that my assistant, Beth Nelson, and I could easily assist the teams as they became familiar with these procedures.

I first worked with Nelson during the summers of 1982 and 1983 at a small shell midden site off Ryder's Cove in Chatham; she had studied anthropology and archaeology in college. As my assistant on this project, Nelson's responsibility was to direct the crew in establishing transects to be used in testing the island.

At mid-morning, we left the lab and headed out to Wing Island. The early morning fog had burned off and the hot sun was overhead. Once on the island, we followed the trail to the small field near the center of the island. This was our starting point. The Brewster Conservation Commission maintains this field habitat to encourage the growth of several endangered wildflower species that would otherwise be crowded out by the reforestation of the island. I chose to begin our work in this field because it was open and could be tested in a relatively short period of time. Once at the field, we quickly located one of the wooden stakes established in the survey. From that point, we created a series of north/south running transects throughout the field. Sixty shovel test pits were staked out at five-meter intervals along these lines. The test pits located in this small field would provide us with our first glimpse of the archaeology of the island.

By late morning, the crew had begun excavating the first test pits of the project. While the crew carefully worked, Beth and I discussed the depth of the pits. On Cape Cod, shovel test pits are usually excavated to a depth of the "glacial surface," which is characterized by the presence of coarse quartz sand and "ventifacts," stones shaped and polished by wind-blown sand. Ventifacts were created as they lay atop the unvegetated surface of the Cape after the retreat of the ice 18,000 years ago. As the climate warmed and plants returned to the region, soils began to develop on the glacial surface. The depth of soil formation varies across the Cape, but in most cases the glacial surface lies less than a meter below the current surface of the ground. It is in the soils above the glacial surface that we find evidence of human activity. When excavating a shovel test pit, the glacial surface represents an important marker.

Fred Dunford and crew members examine a shovel test pit.

By noon of the second day, we had excavated about eight or nine shovel test pits. The air was heavy and rain was threatening. In most of our test pits, the glacial surface was found 60cm–70cm below the ground surface. By carefully examining the soils within each test unit, we also discovered that the field had been plowed during the last century. This observation, determined by an even separation of the "A" and "B" horizons, was significant for two reasons. First, we knew that men like Rennie and Crowell previously had scoured the fields of Stony Brook Valley searching for artifacts. Had they searched this field, and if so, what had they found? Second, the plowing of any archaeological site disturbs the area, making it difficult to reconstruct prehistoric activities. But so far we had only discovered a few rusted nails and other bits of metal. For some crew members, the enthusiasm of the first day was starting to wane.

By early afternoon, it was raining. While the rain was a welcome relief, it complicated our work, soaking field forms and turning the silty soil in the screen to mud. But this misery was short-lived. A crew member called out to Beth and me to see what he had found. There in the screen were several pieces of chipping debris. To an untrained eye, these small, thumbnail-size flakes might look unimpressive, but to us they provided an answer: Wing Island had been occupied, or at least used, by native peoples several thousand years ago. We had found a prehistoric site, although we weren't certain how old it was.

The size and thinness of the flakes indicated they were the result of re-sharpening or finishing stone tools. The absence of large flakes or flakes with a cortex (the surface, or weathered, rind of a rock) indicated that stone tools had not been made here. Large flakes, or flakes with a cortex, are usually found at places where large rocks like beach cobbles had been collected and broken up with stone hammers, creating large flakes for use.

For the rest of the first week and all of the second week, we continued to test the field, excavating a total of 60 test pits and recovering about 80 pieces of chipping debris. At the end of each day, we plotted the distribution of these artifacts on a site map, with the hopes of discerning some pattern. But there was none. Plowing had obviously disturbed the site, spreading the artifacts across the field. No pottery or stone tools had been recovered. Did this mean the site had been occupied before clay vessels were used? We weren't certain. In addition, we were frustrated because we hadn't found any diagnostic stone tools—spear points or other implements of a known age—that might help date the site. These 60 shovel test pits, the first of hundreds we would dig on the island, raised far more questions than they answered.

Having completed the testing of the field, I divided the crew into two groups. One group was assigned to establish a transect from Station D, an oak stake just south of the

Pictured above Fred Dunford walks along a transect giving instructions to crew members.

Below a crew member uses a three-meter tape to record the dimensions of a shovel test pit.

field. This transect would run west from that point to the western edge of the island. It was our hope the transect would pass through the area that had once contained saltworks. We knew from historical accounts that by the mid-19th century when the salt industry began to decline, wood was scarce on the Cape. Indeed, an 1870 photograph of the island shows a barren landscape. As the industry declined because more efficient sources of salt were available, the saltworks fell into disrepair and wood from the vats and other structures were used to construct buildings elsewhere. While we didn't expect to find any wood in the thick brush, we thought we would find nails and other debris.

The second group was moved farther south along the trail to Station C to lay out a transect to the eastern edge of the island. Anticipation was high because this line would run parallel to the field we had identified a prehistoric site.

In both areas, the pace of work was slow. Dense vegetation made the job of creating transects difficult. One member of the crew held the end of the tape on the wooden stake, using a compass to site the line, directing the rest of the team where to cut. The lines were extended 20–40 meters at a time. Every five meters, a flag was placed marking the location of a test pit. Test units were established, then excavated.

By early August we were nearing the end of the first field season. The results of our testing on the western side of the island were discouraging. It was obvious the field season would end before reaching the salt marsh. Other than rusted nails, few traces of the saltworks had been discovered. We understood why we hadn't recovered any wood, but why, given what appeared to be an ambitious industry on Wing Island, was there so little evidence of the saltworks?

I decided to look again at the 1868 map. Specifically, I searched for topographic features in the area where saltworks were shown on the map. This, I thought, might help identify the exact location of the salt works. I plotted transect D against topographic features shown on the map. This was a tricky process because the scale we used to survey the island differed from the scale used in 1868. We were mapping in five-meter intervals, roughly about 15 feet, while the old map was drawn at a much larger scale. In laying out our transect on the map, I determined it had passed just south of the salt works. We would now have to establish a north-running transect to pass directly through the area where the saltworks had stood in the last century.

Even with the availability of good historical sources, the search for subsurface archaeological sites is always a challenge.

SOME ENCOURAGEMENT

However, the results from test pits on transect C, on the eastern side of the island, were far more encouraging. After completing about 10 test pits along that line, we had found another prehistoric site. Small amounts of chipping debris were uncovered about 80 meters east of the path. To define the boundaries of this site, we decided to lay out shovel test pits on transects south of transect C. Only weeks remained in the field season, and we were eager to determine the age of this site. We would not have long to wait.

We gathered at the lab on the morning of August 15. As we did each morning, Beth and I reviewed procedures and updated the group about various aspects of the project. The crew was showing the strain and frustration of the tedious search and the daily battle with bullbriers and poison ivy. To lighten the mood, I had taped a Calvin and Hobbes cartoon to the blackboard behind my desk. It simply illustrated the optimism one needed for these types of projects. In the cartoon, Hobbes hovers over a hole in the ground that Calvin is digging.

"Why are you digging a hole?" Hobbes asks.

"I'm looking for buried treasure," Calvin replies from inside the pit.

"What have you found?"

"A few dirty rocks, a weird root and some disgusting grubs."

"On your first try?"

"There's treasure everywhere!" Calvin replies with delight.

With such encouragement, we left the lab for the island. One of the students, Josiah Campbell, seemed particularly engaged in his work that day. Campbell had just completed his senior year at Nauset High School in North Eastham where he had been class president; he would be leaving in a few weeks to attend Franklin Pierce College in New Hampshire to study anthropology. He was intent on making a major contribution to the project. Ultimately, he did. Two hours into the day, he called out to me. As I walked east on transect C, he yelled with excitement, "We found it!"

"Found what?" I shot back, pushing through the brush to the test pit where Campbell stood.

He held out two plastic artifact bags. One of them contained chipping debris and the tip of a finely-flaked stone spear point. Campbell had carefully written on the outside of the bag that the spear point tip had been found in "level 3" of the test pit, about 30 centimeters deep. Campbell opened the second bag and retrieved the base of a spear point recovered at 40 centimeters. He took the two and held them in his hand. They fit together perfectly.

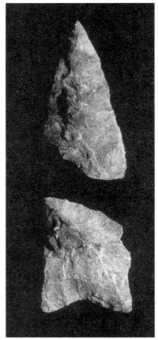

These two photographs show two pieces of a finely flaked 4,000 year old stone spear point—the first significant artifact found during the course of the Wind Island survey.

As he held the pieces together, I looked for any indication of how this thin spear point had been broken. Along the edge of the blade, where the crack originated, was a small nick. As the point was being sharpened, probably by someone using a pressure flaker (a pointed tool made from a deer antler), the blade had cracked and had been discarded. But more important than knowing how this artifact had been broken, we knew how old it was. The edges at the base of the blade had been notched and ground so the stone point could be hafted to the wooden foreshaft of a spear. This technology was used by native peoples in the region about 4,000 years ago. Now we knew! The island had been used by native peoples at least 4,000 years ago.

In the remaining two weeks, we recovered more than 10 other stone tools from the gentle slope just south of transect C and copious quantities of chipping debris and small fragments of burned animal bone, thereby establishing the area south of transect C as an important site of prehistoric activity.

There would be more surprises. One afternoon in the base of a test pit, we found a broken spear point dating back 8,000 years along with two unbroken spear points about 4,000 years old.

Why an 8,000-year-old artifact would be found alongside a 4,000-year-old artifact is not so much a mystery. Insects, such as ants, can churn a foot of sandy soil every thousand years, mixing and moving artifacts up and down through soil horizons, presenting challenges for archaeologists.

But discovery of the 8,000-year-old artifact raised many questions. The Run Hill Road Site at Upper Mill Pond, just a mile south of the island, had been occupied at the same time.

Were the people who lived along this gentle south-facing slope 8,000 years ago the same people who camped on the eastern shore of Upper Mill Pond? What attracted these people to the island? Did they come here in the spring to fish for alewives in Paine's Creek? Or did they travel here for some other reason? The answer to these and other intriguing questions would have to wait for future field seasons.

TESTING THE SALT MARSH

While we were conducting the archaeological investigation of the island, a team of geologists from Brown University, under the direction of Dr. Thompson Webb III and Paige Newby, was exploring the salt marsh. Because we assumed that the island had been home to native peoples thousands of years before the arrival of Wing, Dillingham and the others, we had arranged for this team of geologists and palynologists to assist us in reconstructing the environment before the 17th century. Of specific interest was the timing of the development of the salt marsh. Because most salt marshes on the Cape are less than 4,000

Geologist Robert Oldale (right) watches as geologists from Brown University take a core sample from the salt marsh.

thousand years old, we were curious about the environment that surrounded the island before that time. Supported by a grant from the SEA Grant program at the Woods Hole Oceanographic Institution, the geologists arrived early in August.

Their first task was to determine the depth of the salt marsh peat at various locations across the salt marsh. The salt marsh had developed within a low-lying area—a shallow basin between the upland where the museum sits and the island to the north. To establish the depth of the marsh, geologists established transects east-west and north-south across the salt marsh. They then moved along east transects and, at measured intervals, about 20 meters, used a steel probe one inch in diameter to determine the depth of the peat. After recording a series of measurements, they created a map of the basin within which the marsh had formed. Almost immediately, we were intrigued by the results.

Their testing revealed an extremely sharp drop along the southern margin of the is-land—in some places a depth of more than one meter. After reviewing the data, geologist Robert Oldale of the US Geological Survey headquarters at Woods Hole suggested that the southern side of the island may have been cut by wave action before the development of the salt marsh. The implication suggested that at high tide the basin may have been a shallow lagoon. Another possibility is that before the formation of the marsh, either Paine's Creek or Quivet Creek may have followed a course along the southern side of the island. In either case, these observations have important implications for understanding the adaptation of lifeways of native peoples who occupied the island before the salt marsh was formed. Were they here to fish in the shallow waters of the lagoon at high tide or to set fish weirs in the running water of the tidal creeks?

After gathering information about the basin, the geologists turned their attention to collecting a sample of the peat that would allow them to document historical changes in vegetation. To do this, they took a five-meter core sample in the deepest peat in the marsh, a spot east of the causeway. The results were fascinating. At about 1.5 meters below the present surface of the salt marsh, the coring instrument intersected a thick deposit of fine quartz sand, interpreted by the geologists as dune sand. At some point during the development of the salt marsh, perhaps around 1,000 years ago, a sand dune moved across the salt marsh.

What that meant for natives who relied on the marsh for food and resources is the subject of future testing on Wing Island. As with most archaeological undertakings, the investigation of the salt marsh was far more complex than we had imagined, and raised more questions than were answered.

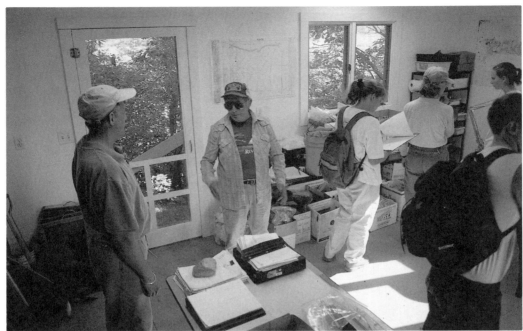

Field crew members organize equipment and receive instructions before heading out to the island in the early morning.

Fred Dunford and field crew members cut a transect through the thick brush on the island.

Field crew members use a 50-meter tape and a compass to layout a transect.

*Crew members excavate a shovel test pit along a narrow transect
cut through the thick brush.*

Photographs of some of the stone spear points recovered during our survey of Wing Island.

The two side-notched spear points on the upper left are about 4,000 years old. The spear point on the upper right is about 6,000 years old. The broken spear point at the bottom is about 8,000 years old. These artifacts provide a general chronology for the prehistoric occupation of the island. Research to date tells us when native peoples occupied the island. Now, we will search to find out what brought them here.

1996 FIELD SEASON

During the 1996 field season, we continued to discover evidence of the occupation of the island by native peoples during the last several thousand years. To date, more than 500 shovel test pits have been excavated on Wing Island. We have recovered hundreds of pieces of chipping debris and about 40 stone tools—spear points, scrapers and drills. Of great continuing interest is the fact that Wing Island and the nearby Run Hill Road site were occupied at the same time, although the nature of the two sites appears to be different. The site at Upper Mill Pond that we excavated between 1987 and 1990 is a relatively small campsite that seems to have been occupied for a very short period of time. The prehistoric site on the southern side of Wing Island is fairly extensive and has yielded a diversity of stone tools, dating to the period between 8,000 and 4,000 years ago. Wing Island appears to have been a very important place for native peoples. Our work in the years to come will be directed toward learning what attracted people to the island so many thousands of years ago.

What else have we learned about the archaeology of the island?

During the summer of 1996, we ran a transect oriented to north, directly through the area where the 1868 map showed the location of the saltworks. The results have proved to be very interesting. We found virtually no subsurface evidence of the saltworks, with the exception of numerous rusty nails and other bits of iron. This seems to suggest (although our conclusions are preliminary) that the saltworks structures were built on wooden frames placed on the surface of the ground.

In addition, our failure to find any wood from the saltworks seems to confirm the theory that the saltworks were dismantled after 1870 and the wood was taken off the island for use in other projects. During the next several field seasons, we will continue to search for evidence of the saltworks industry on Wing Island.

What about John Wing?

Our search to date has also failed to provide any evidence of Wing's occupation of Wing Island, but a considerable portion of the island remains to be tested. Evidence of Wing's homestead may be discovered in the years to come.

It is now February 1997, and as I look out from the lab across the marsh to the island, I think about John Wing, the history of the island, and about the many secrets that await discovery in the years to come.

John Hay must be pleased.

"Visited and possessed by the outer sea, these sands might be the end or the beginning of a world."
—HENRY BESTON, THE OUTERMOST HOUSE

Life of the Nauset People: Text as Artifacts

In July of 1605, French explorer Samuel de Champlain sailed his barque into the shallow waters of Nauset Inlet. In his journal, he recorded the first European description of a place he named Port de Mallebarre, which today lies on the eastern edge of the Town of Eastham.

Wrote Champlain:

> The next day, the 20th of the month, we went to the place which our men had seen, and which we found a very dangerous harbor in consequence of the shoals and banks, where we saw breakers in all directions. It was almost low tide when we entered, and there were only four feet of water in the northern passage; at high tide, there are two fathoms. After we had entered, we found the place very spacious, being perhaps three or four leagues in circuit, entirely surrounded by little houses, around each one of which there was as much land as the occupant needed for his support. A small river enters here, which is very pretty, and which at low tide, there are some three and a half feet of water. There are also two or three brooks bordered by meadows. It would be a very fine place, if the harbor were good. I took the altitude, and found the latitude 42 degrees, and the deflection of the magnetic needle 18 degrees, 40 minutes. Many savages, men and women, visited us, and ran up on all sides, dancing. We named this place Port de Mallebarre.

It is July of 1996, almost 400 years later. The summer birds have arrived. Just off the stern of the *Nauset Explorer*, a motorized catamaran plying the shallows of Nauset Inlet, a squadron of black skimmers flies with precision in search of food. Oystercatchers patrol the tidal edge. In the distance, a northern harrier glides gracefully.

Nearby, the Eldredge brothers rake for mussels, as they have for many years. The supple marsh grass is a rich green. In the distance, you can hear the pounding surf of Nauset Beach. The marsh, on the lip of Orleans and Eastham, is timeless. You can close your eyes in the gentle breeze and imagine what explorer Champlain saw here in the summer of 1605. Those aboard the *Nauset Explorer* have come to do just that.

Several hundred yards off the bow, a meadow rises gently in neighboring Eastham. It is called Fort Hill, and for more than 3,000 years it was home to native peoples; the last settlement here was called Nauset, and a young man named Aspinet was sachem, or political leader, of that community. Shell middens along the shoreline attest to generations of occupation. The middens offer up prehistoric stone tools, pottery, and bones of animals and fish.

I have a copy of Champlain's illustrated map of Fort Hill and Nauset Harbor, showing houses, gardens and fish weirs. In my role as a guide aboard the *Explorer* on this museum-sponsored trip, I share it with the passengers—two young families from Phoenix, the McGeorges and the Artigues. I read to them passages from Champlain's journal:

> The next day, the 21st of the month, Sieur de Monts determined to go and see their habitation. Nine or ten of us accompanied him with our arms; the rest remained to guard the barque. We went about a league along the coast. Before reaching their cabins, we entered a field planted with Indian corn in the manner before described. The corn was in flower and five and a half feet high. There was some less advanced, which they plant later. We saw many Brazilian beans, and many squashes of various sizes, very good for eating; some tobacco, and roots which they cultivate, the latter having the taste of an artichoke. The woods are filled with oaks, nut trees, and beautiful cypresses, which are of a reddish color and have a very pleasant odor.

Champlain described the native peoples he met at Nauset: The people wore

> . . .neither robes, nor furs, except very rarely: morever, there robes are made of grasses and hemp, scarcely covering the body, and coming down only to their thighs. They have only the sexual parts concealed with a small piece of leather; so likewise the women, with whom it comes down a little lower behind than with the men, all the rest of the body being naked. Whenever the women came to see us, they wore robes which were open in front. The men cut off their hair on the top of the head, like those at the river Chouacoet. I saw, among other things, a girl with her hair very neatly dressed, with a skin-colored red, and bordered on the upper part with little shell beads. A part of her hair hung down behind, the rest being graded in various ways. These people paint the face red, black and yellow.

While exploring the waters of the inlet, Champlain saw many of the same creatures we see today.

> In this place . . . there are a great many siguenocs (horseshoe crabs), which is a fish with a shell on its back, like the tortoise, yet different, there being in the middle a row of little prickles, of the color of a dead leaf, like the rest of a fish, at the end of this shell, there is another, still smaller, bordered by very sharp points. The length of the tail varies according to their size. With the end of it, these people point their arrows, and it contains also a row of prickles like the large shell in which are the eyes.

Champlain also described the beautiful black skimmers,

> We saw also a sea-bird with a black beak, the upper part slightly aquiline, four inches long and in the form of a lancet; namely, the lower part representing the handle and the upper the blade, which is thin, sharp on both sides, and shorter by a third than the other, which circumstance is a matter of astonishment to many persons, who cannot comprehend how it is possible for this bird to eat with such a beak."

After recording these marvelous sights, Champlain left Nauset Inlet on July 25, 1605 to sail to Canada. The last journal entry describes his passage across the treacherous shoals of the inlet. Champlain wrote:

> We set out from this harbor in order to make observations elsewhere. In going out, we came near being lost on the bar at the entrance, from the mistake of our pilots, Cramolet and Champdore, masters of the barque, who had imperfectly marked out the entrance of the channel on the southern side, where we were to go. Having escaped this danger, we headed northeast.

The passengers aboard the *Explorer* are fascinated by these eyewitness accounts. They want to know more. "Are these accounts accurate?" they ask. I tell them that archaeologists often use passages like these to better understand the lifeways of the people they are studying. But they must be used carefully. Each account must be critically evaluated— Who wrote it and why? Where was the author from? How does the culture, religion, class and economic status influence the writer's interaction with and description of the native peoples? In a sense, the texts themselves are artifacts. If read critically and objectively, they do indeed provide a revealing picture of the lives of the native peoples who lived along this coast in the 17th century.

The boat rolls gently in the wake of a passing skiff. I fold my copy of Champlain's chart and tell the group to turn and look at the gently sloping meadow of Fort Hill. I tell them to close their eyes and imagine the grass huts and corn fields that stood there in the summer of 1605. In this chapter, we use these and other texts to paint a word picture of life in the community of Nauset 400 years ago.

TEXTS AS ARTIFACTS: WHO WERE THE NAUSET PEOPLE?

The rising sea had begun to define the modern shoreline of Cape Cod by 3,000 years ago, and salt marshes had begun to develop behind barrier beaches like the Nauset barrier spit. The Cape's native peoples gathered seasonally near these bays and salt marshes. Archaeological evidence recovered from the excavation of shell middens at Fort Hill suggests that native peoples were residing along the shores of Nauset Inlet by 3,000 years ago. These were the ancestors of the people who lived in the community of Nauset and met Champlain in the summer of 1605.

The annual occupation of Nauset Inlet in the summer months by groups of related families created an important, historical attachment to that place. The "connectedness" of families to important places on the landscape effectively created community. Therefore, between 3,000 years and 400 years ago, separate communities developed at all of the major bays and estuaries on Cape Cod.

Anthropologists Yves Goddard and Kathleen Bragdon have offered important insight into how these communities developed over time. They theorize that communities "were associated with specific geographic locations well known to the sachems and their followers" and that the members of communities, like Nauset, inherited both membership and land rights. They describe the historical linkage of families or households to a sachem as an "on-going, organic social grouping, to which one's ancestors belonged and to which one's own descendants would be loyal."

The community of Nauset was defined both by territory and politics. By supporting the sachem or "head man" of Nauset, its inhabitants had rights and access to all of the resources surrounding this important estuary system. Plimoth colonist Edward Winslow, who was at one time Governor of the colony, described a sachem's control over his territory.

> Every sachim knoweth how far the bounds and limits of his country extendeth; and that is his own proper inheritance. Out of that, if any of his men desire land to set their corn, he giveth them as much as they can use, and sets them their bounds . . .

152

The sachem was the central, political figure in each community and was typically from one of its more influential families. In addition, a sachem was usually a Pniese. The Pnieses constituted a special group of men, who, as young boys had undergone rigorous training—a sort of vision quest—that endowed them with the powers of Hobbamock, a powerful spirit that appeared to the Pnieses in animal form, protecting and guiding them.

Winslow described the quest to obtain Hobbamock:

> And to the end that they may have store of these, they train up the most forward and likeliest boys, from their childhood, in great hardness, and make them abstain from dainty meat, observing divers orders prescribed, to the end that when they are of age, the devil may appear to them: causing them to drink the juice of sentry and other bitter herbs, till they cast, which they must disgorge into the platter, and drink again and again, till at length through extraordinary oppressing of nature, it will seem to be all blood; and this the boys will do with eagerness at first, and so continue till by reason of faintness they can scarce stand on their legs, and then must go forth into the cold. Also they beat their shins with sticks, and cause them to run through bushes, stumps and brambles, to make them hardy and acceptable to the devil, that in time he may appear unto them.

Winslow's belief that the powerful Hobbamock was the devil of Christianity is an example of the cultural differences between the English and the native peoples of the region. This is why these texts must be read carefully.

After successfully completing this rigorous period of testing and deprivation, the Pnieses obtained Hobbamock and were seen by members of the community as

> . . . Men of great courage and wisdom. To those also the devil appeareth more familiarly than to others and as we can see maketh covenant with them to preserve them from death by wounds, with arrows, knives and hatchets or at least both themselves and especially the people think themselves to be freed from the same. And though, against their battles, all of them by painting disfigure themselves, yet they are known by their courage and boldness, by reason whereof one of them will chase almost an hundred men; for they account it death for whomsoever stand in their way. These are highly esteemed of all sorts of people, and are of the sachim's council, without whom they will not war, or undertake any weighty business.

The sachems then, were not only from the most influential families, but they had undergone important training which in adulthood provided wisdom, strength, courage and strong moral character.

While a son, and in some cases a daughter or a wife, succeeded the father as sachem upon his death, a sachem still had to actively create and maintain a following. Sachems sought the support of families within the community, and families sought those benefits (such as access to planting fields) that a sachem could provide. Families would give sachems corn and other goods, and the sachem would provide in return protection and assistance when necessary. While the sachem accumulated stores of produce and material, he would use these goods to assist families in need. For instance, if a family's garden failed, the sachem would provide corn. Winslow wrote that "Every sachim taketh care for the widow and fatherless, also for such as are aged and any way maimed, if their friends be dead, or not able to provide for them."

At times the sachem would organize a feast for the community. Winslow wrote that after receiving the corn from the households the sachem would give thanks "bestowing many gifts on them."

A sachem had to work to satisfy his followers because they were always free to leave the community or support a challenger. In addition, a sachem never made an important decision without carefully listening to the advice of the village elders or others who might voice an opinion. Winslow offers a unique glimpse of political life in these communities.

> Their sachims have not their men in such subjection but that very frequently their men will leave them upon distaste or harsh dealings, and go and live under other sachems that can protect them; so their princes endeavour to carry it obligingly and lovingly unto their people.

Life within these communities like Nauset, consisted of a daily exchange of favors and goods between households and the sachem. These exchanges cemented the bonds of the community.

Winslow wrote that it was customary for visitors to a community to meet with the sachem to explain the reason for their visit.

> All travellers or strangers for the most part lodge at the sachim's. When they come, they tell them how long they will stay, and to what place they go; during which time they receive entertainment, according to their persons, but want not.

So, in July 1605, as Champlain and his party landed their boat at the foot of the gently sloping meadow we now call Fort Hill, they would have been led through fields and gardens to the dwelling of the sachem. His journal provides an account of his conversation with the native peoples of Nauset:

We asked them if they had their permanent abode in this place and whether there was much snow. But we were unable to ascertain this from them, not understanding their language, although they made an attempt to inform us by signs, by taking some sand in their hands, spreading it out over the ground, and indicating that it was the color of our collars, and that it (snow) reached the depth of a foot. Others made signs that there was less, and gave us to understand also that the harbor never froze; but we were unable to ascertain whether the snow lasted long. I conclude, however, that this region is of moderate temperate, and the weather not severe.

The Nauset people spoke Massachusett, a dialect of the eastern Algonkian language. Massachusett was not a written language. John Eliot, a missionary who created the praying town at Natick, developed a dictionary of Massachusett words. By working with this important dictionary, local historian Warren Sears Nickerson has brought to life many of the Massachusett words which describe places on Cape Cod; Pochet, for example, meant the "dividing place" and signified both a topographical and political divide between Monomoyett and Nauset. Nickerson cites Barnstable historian James Otis in telling us the origin of the word Mattacheesett. He writes, "Otis says the word was compounded of Matta (old or poor when used in this connection), ohkee (ground or fields), ese or ise (a diminutive term meaning little). Mattakeeset the same, with the addition of the terminal et meaning "place" or "here at the place" which our Indians uniformly applied to places near the water. The whites translated it literally to "Old Fields." In other unpublished notes, Nickerson defines the word Moskeetukqut as meaning "the great marshes of Barnstable." (It is interesting to note that Kittredge and his partners in forming their Sandy Neck gunning camp, chose the name "Mosquetucket.)

The inhabitants of Nauset lived in circular houses made of bent saplings which were covered with mats made from salt marsh grasses. The Plimoth colonists found several of these houses as they traveled throughout the area that is now Wellfleet and Truro in November and December of 1620. The occupants, unsure of the intent of the Plimoth company, had gone into hiding. These houses are described in *Mourt's Relation*, the first published account of the Plimoth colonists' arrival and settlement in the New World:

> The houses were made with long, young sapling trees bended and both ends stuck into the ground. They were made round like unto an arbor and covered down to the ground with thick and well wrought mats and the door was not over a yard high made of a mat to open. The chimney was a wide open hole in the top, for which they had a mat to cover it closed when they please. One might stand and go upright in them. In the midst

An artist's rendition of a Wetu like that described in Mourt's Relation.

of them were four little trunches knocked into the ground and small sticks laid over on which they hung their pots and what they had to seeth round about the fire they lay on mats which are their beds. Their houses were double matted for as they were matted without, so were they matted within with newer and fairer mats.

This account also provides a wonderful description of the belongings that the colonists saw within the house.

> And in the houses we found wooden bowls, trays and dishes, earthen pots, handbaskets made of crab shells wrought together. Also an English pail or bucket...there was also baskets of sundry sorts, bigger and some lesser, finer and some corser. Some were curiously wrought with black and white and pretty works and sundry other of their household stuff. We found also two or three deers heads, one whereof had been newly killed for it was still fresh. There was also a company of deers' feet stuck up in the houses, hart's horn and eagle's claws and sundry such like things there was. Also two or three baskets full of parched acorns, pieces of fish and a broiled herring. We found also a little silk grass and a little tobacco seed with some other seeds which we knew not . . . There was thrust into a hollow of a tree two or three pieces of venison, but we thought it fitter for the dogs than us. Some of the best things we took away with us and left the houses standing still as they were. So growing towards night and the tide almost spent we hasted with our things down to the shallop and got aboard that night.

Roger Williams in writing about the Narragansett people who lived in what is now Rhode Island described dwellings which were very similar to those described by Champlain and the Plimoth colonists.

> Two families will live comfortably and lovingly in a little round house of some fourteen or sixteen foot over, and so more and more families in proportion." The houses were constructed of long poles "which commonly men get and fix, and then the women cover the house with mats, and line them with embroydered mats which the women make, and call them 'Mannotaubana, or Hangings,' which amongst them make as faire a show as Hangings with us.

The inhabitants of Nauset came each spring to the area surrounding what is now Fort Hill. The sachem would assign gardens to each family. Houses were then constructed near the gardens. Women and children were primarily responsible for tending the gardens of corn and a variety of other plants, such as those described by Champlain earlier in this chapter.

The soil, before the deforestation and erosion which occurred during the English settlement of the Cape, was exceptionally fertile. Bradford writes, "the ground or earth, sand hils, much like the Downes in Holland, but much better, the crust of the earth a spits depth, excellent blacke earth."

In addition to planting gardens, the women also collected nuts, berries, herbs and other medicinal plants. Bradford provides a vivid account of the woodlands which surrounded Nauset Inlet. The hillsides were "all wooded with Okes, Pines, Sassafras, Juniper, Birch, Holly, Vines, some Ash, Walnut; the wood for the most part open and without underwood, fit either to goe or ride in." The journal also describes plentiful strawberries, blueberries, beach plums and grapes.

Winslow describes the daily activities of women: "The women live a most slavish life; they carry all their burdens, set and dress their corn, gather it in, seek out for much of their food, beat and make ready the corn to eat, and have all the household care lying upon them." In addition to all of these tasks, the women gathered shellfish, crabs and lobsters from the shallow waters of the inlet. Salt marsh grasses were harvested to make mats and baskets.

According to Winslow, "The men employ themselves wholly in hunting, and other exercises of the bow, except at some times they take some pains in fishing." A wide variety of animals, some of which are extinct on Cape Cod, were hunted. The bones of deer, bear, wolves, rabbits, squirrels, and numerous other species have been found in the shell middens surrounding Fort Hill. While both the bow and arrow and spears were used in the hunt, the native peoples of Cape Cod fashioned very effective snares and traps. One such trap snared a member of the Plimoth party during the first exploration of the Cape.

> As we wandered we came to a tree, where a yong Spritt was bowed downe over a bow, and some Acornes strewed underneath; Stephen Hopkins said it had beene to catch some deere, so, as we were looking at it, William Bradford being in the Reare, when he came looked also upon it, and as he went about, it gave a sodaine jerk up, and he was immediately caught by the leg; It was a very pretie devise, made with a Rope of their owne making, and having a noose as artificially made, as any Roper in England can make.

Fishing also involved some sophisticated technology. Wooden canoes were made from large pine logs that had been hollowed out. The bones of fish, such as swordfish which are normally found offshore, suggest that the native peoples of Cape Cod were both excellent seamen and fishermen. Other fish were caught in weirs placed strategically at the mouths of tidal creeks or on the flats of the Bay. Fish, such as sturgeon, were hunted by torch light in the night.

The fall was a season of great activity as the households at Nauset prepared for the long winter ahead. The corn was harvested, dried and stored in pits. In his journal, Champlain described this process:

> All the inhabitants of this place are very fond of agriculture, and provide themselves with Indian corn for the winter, which they store in the following manner: They make trenches in the sand on the slope of the hills, some five to six feet deep, more or less. Putting their corn and other grains into large grass sacks, they throw them into these trenches, and cover them with sand three or four feet above the surface of the earth, taking it out as their needs require. In this way, it is preserved as well as it would be possible to do in our granaries.

Cooking and storage pots were made from clay that was collected along the shore of the inlet. The pots were stored for use during the winter, a time when the weather prevented the community from making pots. Acorns and other nuts would be gathered and dried. The men prepared themselves for the fall hunt. When everything was ready, the community broke up into family groups and moved to the protected shores of kettlehole ponds to weather the worst of the winter months.

During the winter, small groups would often return to the shores of the inlet to collect shellfish. Shellfish were an important winter food and were available when many other foods were not. Baskets of shellfish could be taken back to the winter camp where they could be stored in snow banks.

I conclude the stories by telling the group that the people of Nauset and the other native communities of the Cape lived close to the earth, following the rhythms of seasonal change, rhythms that call out to us today.

It is now time to return to the dock. The captain fires up the engine and noses the bow back toward Town Cove. The group is quiet, perhaps reflecting on the lives of those who walked these shores hundreds of years ago.

I stand near the stern watching Fort Hill fade in the distance. I think about the story I have just told—weaving together historical accounts and archaeological research. I am reminded of what John Hanson Mitchell wrote in his book, *Ceremonial Time*, about the magic of the mind's eye. Wrote Mitchell:

> I found that when the moment was right, by concentrating on some external object, an arrowhead . . . for example . . . I was able to perceive something more than a simple mental picture of what some past event was like. I not only could see the event or place in my mind's eye, but would also hear it, smell the wood fires; and sometimes, for just a micro-second if you care to measure things, I would actually be there, or so it seemed.

There have been rare moments in the last 15 years of field work that I have experienced what Mitchell described. In the summer of 1988, as I brushed sand away from the burned cobbles of the ancient hearth at Upper Mill Pond, I tried to picture the native peoples who sat by that fire 8,000 years ago. Who were they? What were they thinking, as they looked out across the quiet waters of the pond? Although we were separated by thousands of years, our lives were connected in that instant.

It is late afternoon when the *Nauset Explorer* slips up against the dock in Town Cove. The passengers depart. Meanwhile, out on the marsh, the skimmers continue to search for food, and the Eldredge brothers are still hard at work. The sun has started to sink toward the horizon.

Tomorrow morning we will be back at Wing Island, renewing our search for secrets in the sand.

Glossary

"A" and "B" Soil Horizons: To describe soil development in a given area, scientists use a sequence of lettered soil horizons, or layers. Leaf litter or humus is on the surface of Cape soil. Below that is the "A" horizon—a dark brown-to-black soil high in organic matter. At the base of the "A" horizon, is a bone-white horizon where percolating water has leached the iron oxides out of the soil, depositing them in the "B" horizon below and forming an orange-brown rust stain on the course sand.

Archaic Period: The Archaic Period spans the millennia between 9,500 to about 2,500 years and is divided by early, middle and late periods. Native peoples who lived in the region during this period were hunter-gatherer-fishers.

Assemblage: A group of artifacts found at the same site.

Artifact: Portable objects used made or modified by people, such as stone spear points, clay pots and bone needles.

Bifaces: Stone tools that have been flaked on both faces, such as spear or arrow points.

Blowouts: Places within a dune where wind or erosion has uncovered buried land surfaces.

Chipping debris: thin flakes of stone that are the by-products or waste from making stone tools.

Cooking Stones: Rocks heated by fire that were placed in a clay pot to boil the liquid contents of the pot.

Feature: A non-portable artifact, such as a trash pit or a hearth.

Fluted Spear Point: An artifact that characterized Paleoindian toolkits. A "fluted" point is a bifacially flaked (flaked on both sides) spear or projectile point, with a flake scar usually on both faces of the blade. The flake starts at the base of the point and extends toward the mid-point of the blade. Some archaeologists have argued that once impaled, a "grooved" blade caused animals to bleed excessively—which was critical in subduing animals much larger than the hunter. Some have suggested that flaking a blade in this manner was part of the process of hafting, or connecting, the blade to the shaft of the spear. Others have insisted the "fluting" a spear or projectile point was simply part of the broader lithic technology (stone tool technology) of Paleoindians, a trait consistent within Paleoindian groups across the continent.

Glacial Surface: A surface characterized by the presence of coarse quartz sand and ventifacts, stones shaped and polished by windblown sand and silt. Ventifacts were created as they lay atop the unvegetated surface of the Cape after the retreat of the ice 18,000 years ago. As the climate warmed and plants returned to the region, soils began to develop on the glacial surface. The depth of soil formation varies across the Cape, but in most cases the glacial surface lies less than a meter below the current surface of the ground.

Grid: A geometric arrangement of excavation units across an excavation area. A grid allows archaeologists to precisely map the location of artifacts.

Hammer Stone: A fist-sized cobble used in the production and maintenance of stone tools, a process generally referred to as flint knapping.

Middens (or shell middens or shell heaps): Refuse deposits of varying sizes that consist primarily of discarded prehistoric shell, plant and animal remains, broken stone and bone tools and other household items. The presence of great quantities of shell neutralizes the acidity of the soil, preserving important information about prehistoric environments, resources and the implements made and used by native people.

Lithic Analysis: Study of stone tools.

Lithic Artifacts: Objects made of stone.

Paleoindians: Small bands of hunter-gatherers who between 12,000 and 13,000 years ago crossed the windswept steppes of Siberia, across a land bridge at the Bering Strait, to enter North America. Within a thousand years, these people, now called Paleoindians by archaeologists (from Paleolithic-Old Stone Age and Indian) had colonized all of North and South America.

Palynologists: Scientists who explore the relationship between climate and the environment by examining historical changes in forest composition. To do this, they collect and study pollen grains that have been trapped within the sediments of ponds, bogs and marshes. The preservation of fossil pollen grains within soils and wetland sediments provides an important data base for examining climatic and environmental change.

Parabolic Dunes: U shaped sand dunes with the open end facing the wind. They are formed when the wind blows away the sand at the middle of an existing dune, sometimes exposing the underlying beach deposits, and drops it downwind along the advancing leeward face of the dune. Parabolic dunes can be seen in the Province Lands of the Cape Cod National Seashore.

Patination: Weathering that occurs to stone artifacts buried in the ground for long periods of time. The acidity of the soil causes the outer surface of the artifacts to fade in color as the stone is weathered.

Plummets: Teardrop-shaped stone weights used to sink fishing nets and lines.

Preforms: Oval or tear drop shaped stone artifacts that represent a mid-stage in making spear points.

Projectile Point: General category referring to both spear and arrow points.

Saltworks: Technology involving wooden vats that was once used to extract salt from seawater through a process of evaporation.

Sherd: A piece of ceramic pottery.

Shovel Scraping: Using a flat shovel with a long handle to scrape in an even manner across the floor of the excavation unit. Done properly, the shovel functions as an extension of the hand, much the way a trowel and brush are used.

Site: Any place on the landscape that provides material evidence of past human activity.

Stratigraphy: The study of stratification—the sequential layers [vertical] or archaeological material, oldest at the bottom and youngest at the top. These layers reveal the history of occupation at an archaeological site.

Stratification: See stratigraphy.

Temper: Additives to clay paste used to make pots that enhanced various physical properties of the vessels. The choice of temper was an important clue in determining the age of these vessels. On Cape Cod, shell temper was first used about a thousand years ago, while crushed quartz or granite temper was used much earlier when native peoples were first experimenting with this new technology.

Walkover: A search on foot for visible archaeological sites.

Wet Screening: A process of using a fine spray to wash the backdirt from the excavation units through a window screen. This process allows for the recovery of exceptionally small objects.

Wetus: Small circular houses made of a framework of bent saplings and covered with mats of saltmarsh grasses.

Woodland Period: Woodland Period covers the years between 2,500 to about 500 years ago. During the Woodland Period, agriculture was added to the subsistence base, in addition to hunting, gathering and fishing.

Bibliography

INTRODUCTION

Beade, Lisa R. *A Portrait of Singular Style — Provincetown Painter Ross Moffet (1888–1971)*. Cape Cod Life. Vol. 18, #2. (1996): p. 38.

Bullen, Ripley P. "Culture Dynamics in Eastern Massachusetts." *American Antiquity*, 14:36-48, 1948.

Carpenter, Delores Bird. *Early Encounters — Native Americans and Europeans In New England*. East Lansing, Mich: Michigan State University Press, 1994.

Del Deo, Josephine C. *Figures in a Landscape, the Life and Times of the American Painter, Ross Moffett, 1888-1971*. Virginia Beach, VA: The Donning Company/Publishers, 1975.

Eteson, Marie, Marilyn D. Crary and Mary F. Chase. "The Mattaquason Purchase Site" [M48NG] North Chatham. *Bulletin of the Massachusetts Archaeological Society* 39:1-38, 1978.

Finch, Robert. *The Woodlands, Heaths and Grasslands, A Guide to Nature on Cape Cod and the Islands*. Hyannis, MA: Parnassus Imprints, 1995.

Freeman, Frederick. *History of Cape Cod: The Annals Of Barnstable County, including the District of Mashpee, Volumes 2 and 3*. Cornhill: George C. Rand and Avery, 1858.

Hyder, Clyde Kenneth. *George Lyman Kittredge: Teacher and Scholar*. Lawrence, KS: University of Kansas Press, 1962.

Magennis, Ann L. *Diet, Nutrition, and Health of the Indian Neck Population, The Indian Neck Ossuary, Chapters in the Archaeology of Cape Cod, V.*, edited by Francis P. McManamon. Boston, MA: Division of Cultural Resources, North Atlantic Cultural Regional Office, National Park Service, 1986.

McManamon, Francis P. *Chapters in the Archaeology of Cape Cod, Volumes 1 and 2*, edited by Francis P. McManamon. Boston, MA: Division of Cultural Resources, North Atlantic Cultural Regional Office, National Park Service, 1984.

McManamon, Francis P.; Bradley, James W. and Magennis, Ann L. The Indian Neck Ossuary, Chapters in the Archaeology of Cape Cod, V., edited by Francis P. McManamon. Boston, MA: Division of Cultural Resources, North Atlantic Cultural Regional Office, National Park Service, 1986.

Moffett, Rose. *A Review of Cape Cod Archaeology.* Bulletin of the Massachusetts Archaeological Society, 19:1-19, 1957.

Nickerson, Warren Sears. *Some Lower Cape Cod Indians.* Eastham, MA: Manuscript on file at the Cape Cod National Seashore, 1933.

Nickerson, Warren Sears. *The Bay As I See It.* Harwich, MA: Jack Viall, 1981.

Paine, Josiah. *History of Harwich.* Hyannis, MA: Parnassus Imprints, 1971.

Smith, Benjamin L. "Toward A Chronology for Massachusetts." Bulletin of the Massachusetts Archaeological Society, 7:49, 1946.

Thoreau, Henry David. *Cape Cod.* New York: Thomas V. Crowell Company, 1961.

Willoughby, Charles C. *Antiquities of the New England Indians.* Cambridge, MA: Peabody Museum of Archaeology and Ethnology, Harvard University, 1935.

LOOKING BACK

Dincauze, D.F. and M.L. Curran. "Paleoindians as Generalists: An Ecological Perspective." Paper presented at the Forty-Eighth Annual Meeting of the Society of American Archaeology, Pittsburgh, PA, 1983.

Emerson, Everett H., ed. *Mourt's Relation.* New York, NY: Garrett Press, Inc., 1969.

Flannery, Kent V. *Origins and Ecological Effects of Early Domestication in Iran and the Near East, Prehistoric Agriculture,* edited by Stuart Struever, pp. 50-79. Garden City, NJ: American Museum Source Books in Anthropology, The Natural History Press, 1971.

MacCurdy, George Grant, ed. *Early Man.* New York, NY: J.B. Lippincott Company, 1937.

FIRST PEOPLE OF THE NARROW LAND

Oldale, Robert N. *Cape Cod and the Islands, the Geologic Story.* Hyannis, MA: Parnassus Imprints, 1992.

LIGHT FROM A DISTANT FIRE

Dunford, Frederick J. "Workshops, Hunting Stands or Huts." Paper presented at the Annual Meeting of the Massachusetts Archaeological Society, North Attleboro, MA, 1988.

Dwight, Timothy. *Travels in New England and New York.* New Haven, CT: S. Converse Printer, 1822.

Hay, John. *The Run.* New York, NY: W.W. Norton and Company, 1959.

SANDY NECK

Barghoorn, Elso and Alfred Redfield. "Palynological Studies of the Barnstable Marsh." *Ecology* Vol. 40, No. 4 (1959).

Bradford, William. *Of Plimoth Plantation.* Boston, MA: Wright and Potter Printing Company, 1900.

Brooks, Edward. "Field Notes." Manuscript on file at the R.S. Peabody Museum for Archaeology, Andover, Ma. (1932).

Bullen, Ripley P. and Edward Brooks. "Shell Heaps on Sandy Neck, Barnstable Massachusetts." Bulletin of the Massachusetts Archaeological Society, Vol. 10, No. 1 (1948).

Dwight, Timothy. *Travels in New England and New York.* New Haven, CT: S. Converse Printer, 1822.

Gibb, George S. "Dr. Lombard Carter Jones: Physician and Indian Votary." Bulletin of the Massachusetts Archaeological Society 50: 67–69 (1989).

Kittredge, Henry. *Cape Cod: Its People and their History.* Boston, MA: Houghton and Mifflin Company, 1930.

McLaughlin, James F., ed. "Proprietor's Records." Town of Barnstable, Barnstable Planning Board, 1703–1795.

Oldale, Robert N. *Cape Cod and the Islands, the Geologic Story.* Hyannis, MA: Parnassus Imprints, 1992.

O'Brien, Greg. *A Guide to Nature on Cape Cod and the Islands.* Excerpt from "The Wetlands by Richard LeBlond, p. 109. Hyannis, MA: Parnassus Imprints, 1995.

Powell, Bernard W. "An Archaeological Traverse of Sandy Neck." Bulletin of the Massachusetts Archaeological Society, Vol. 28, No. 2 (1967).

Redfield, Alfred. "Development of a New England Salt Marsh." *Ecological Monographs*, Vol. 42, No. 2, Woods Hole Oceanographic Institution, Woods Hole, MA (1972).

Svenson, Henry K. *A Linden (Tilia) Forest on Cape Cod* (with extended notes on Tilia Neglecta, Bromus Pubescens and Ribes Hirtellum). Rhodoka, Vol 72, No. 791, 1970.

Teal, John and Mildred. *Life and Death of the Salt Marsh*. New York, NY: Ballantine Books, 1969.

POCHET: ARCHAEOLOGICAL INVESTIGATIONS

de Champlain, Samuel. *Voyages of Samuel De Champlain—1604–1618*. Grant, W.L., ed. New York, N.Y: Charles Scribner and Sons, 1907.

Goddard Ives and Kathleen Bragdon (editors and translators). *Native Writings in Massachusetts*. Memoir No. 185. Philadelphia, PA: American Philosophical Society, 1988.

Nickerson, Warren Sears. *The Bay As I See It*. Harwich, MA: Jack Viall, 1981.

Sargent, William. *Shallow Waters: A Year on Cape Cod's Pleasant Bay*. Boston, MA: Houghton Mifflin Company, 1981.

Young, Alexander, ed. *Chronicles of the Pilgrim Fathers of the Colony of Plymouth, From 1602-1625*. Boston, MA: Charles C. Little and James Brown, 1841.

SOLVING THE MYSTERIES OF WING ISLAND

Perry, Janine M. and Fred Dunford. "Brewster Beginnings: Paine's Creek – Stony Brook Valley." Brewster, MA: Brewster Board of Trade, 1992.

LIFE OF THE NAUSET PEOPLE

Chaplin, Howard M., ed. *A Key Into the Language of America*. Providence, RI: The Roger Williams Press, E.A. Johnson Co., 1936.

Emerson, Everett H., ed. *Mourt's Relation*. New York, NY: Garrett Press, Inc., 1969.

Mitchell, John Hanson. *Ceremonial Time*. Boston, MA: Houghton Mifflin Company, 1984.

Trumbull, James Hammond. "Natick Dictionary." Smithsonian Institution, Bureau of Ethnology, Bulletin 25 (1903).

Index

Page numbers in italics represent illustrations.

Magennis, Dr. Anne, 22.

Maps, *xv, 32, 37, 48, 50, 55, 58, 76,* 98, 123, 131.

Massachusett (language), 155.

Mattaquason (Old Sagamore), sachem, 15, 99.

McManamon, Dr. Francis P., 20.

Mitchell, John Hanson, 159–160.

Moffett, Ross, 19–20.

Monomoyick Indians, 10, 14–15, 99, 100.

Monomoy Island, Chatham MA, 51, *75,* 97.

Monomoymick River, 11, 99.

Monomoyick Tribal Lands, 11, 100.

Moorehead, Warren K., 10.

Nauset Beach, 51, *75,* 81, 97, 150.

Nauset, Eastham, MA, 89.

Nauset Explorer, 149–150, 160.

Nauset (Nawsett) Indians, 4, 14, 10, 99, 100.

Nauset Marsh, 49, 82.

Nauset settlement, 149-160.
  language, 155.
  culture, 152–155, *156,* 158–159.
    sachem, described, 152–154.
  written accounts in *Mourt's Relation,* 155–157.
  written accounts of Edward Winslow, 152–154, 158.
  written accounts of John Hanson Mitchell, 159.
  written accounts of Samuel de Champlain, 149–152, 154–155, 159.

Nelson, Beth, 115, *133,* 134, 136.

Newby, Paige, 141.

Nickerson, Warren Sears, 7, 10, 11, 14, 14–15, 96, 99–100, 155.

Nobscussett Indians, 15.

Oldale, Robert, 33, *40,* 45, 81, *142,* 143.

ossuary, 22.

Otis, James, 155.

Paine, Josiah, 4.

Paine's Creek, 122, 126, 128, 129, 143.

Paleoindians, 26, 28–30.
  and environment on Cape Cod, 30–33.
  and Pleistocene animals as food source, 28, 29.
  archaeological evidence on Cape Cod, 33.
  artifacts, *27,* 28, 29, 33.
  social organization, 29.

parabolic dunes, *51–52.*

patination, 63.

Perry, Janine, 125, 126.

Pleasant Bay, 4, 9, 10, 11, *12,* 13, 15, 40, 41, 49, 97, 99, 100, 101, 110.

Pnieses, 153.

Pochet site (Krusen-Rainey site), East Orleans, MA, 97–118, *114.*
  artifacts, 100, 101, 103, *104,* 115, *117.*
  cultural and environmental interpretation, 115–118.
  discovery, 100–106.
  excavation, *102,* 106–115, *114.*
    observations, 110.
    strategy and methods, 106–110, *107, 109, 111, 112.*
  historical and archaeological background, 97.
  map, 98
  shell middens, 97, 100, 101, 106, *113,* 115, 118.

pottery sherds, 3, 17, 78
  at Pochet, 101, *104, 110.*
    determining age, 103.
  at Wing Island site, 122.

Powell, Bernard, 86, 95.

Pre-Algonkian Period, 16.

Quivet Creek, 122, 126, 128, 143.

radiocarbon dating, 31, 41, 62, 66, 85, 108, 109.

Rainey, Gail, 101, 105, 110.